Phonics and Spelling

Ages 4–5

Julie Crimmins-Crocker

Published by Collins
An imprint of HarperCollins*Publishers*
77–85 Fulham Palace Road
Hammersmith
London
W6 8JB

**Browse the complete Collins catalogue at
www.collinseducation.com**

© HarperCollins*Publishers* Limited 2011, on behalf of the author.
First published in 2007 by Folens Limited.

ISBN-13: 978-0-00-745232-3

British Library Cataloguing in Publication Data
A catalogue record for this publication is available from the British Library.

Every effort has been made to trace copyright holders and to obtain their permission for the use of
copyright material. The authors and publishers will gladly receive any information enabling them to
rectify any error or omission in subsequent editions.

Managing editor: Joanne Mitchell
Editor: Daniel Bottom
Layout artist: Neil Hawkins, ndesignuk.co.uk
Illustrations: JB Illustrations; Jeremy Bays of Art-Work-Shop Graphic Design and Illustration;
Geoff Ball, Helen Jackson and Nicola Pearce of SGA; Tony Randell and Leonie Shearing c/o
Lucas Alexander Whitley.
Cover design for this edition: Julie Martin
Design and layout for this edition: Linda Miles, Lodestone Publishing
Printed and bound in Italy by L.E.G.O. S.p.A., Lavis (TN)

Contents

This contents list provides an overview of the learning objectives of each puzzle page.

Tips for parents

 Read through the title, introduction and instructions for each puzzle to ensure your child knows what to do.

 Point to the phonemes and words covered in the puzzle.

 Demonstrate what the phonemes and words look like and sound like.

 Let your child practise saying the phonemes, blending the phonemes and saying the words in each puzzle.

 Relate the phonemes to other words they know, for example, items in the classroom and at home that also have the same phoneme, rhyme, first phoneme, last phoneme and so on.

 Give your child practise writing the phonemes using a range of materials, for example, sand, whiteboards, crayons, paints and Plasticine.

 Let your child practise writing the phonemes 'in the air' and with pencil and paper, ensuring correct pencil grip and sitting posture.

 Provide additional support if your child needs it, by filling in letters and/or more challenging words/answers.

 After each puzzle go to 'What's next?' (see page 4) and cross off the completed activity. Let your child choose the next one.

Synonym: the same or similar meaning, for example, *big – large*.

Antonym: the opposite meaning, for example, *big – small*.

Anagram: the word is muddled up, for example, *GREAL – LARGE*.

Informal: the word is simple or slang, for example, *rabbit – bunny*.

Verbs are action and 'doing' words, for example, *run*, *talk* and *think*.

Nouns are naming words, for example, *pen*, *hat*, *apple* and *school*.

Adjectives are describing words, for example, *small* bird.

Adverbs add more information to verbs, for example, He ran *quickly*.

Phoneme: a letter or letters that create a single sound when said aloud, for example, **TH** and **OO**.

Letter string: a collection of phonemes, for example, **ELL**.

Vowels are the letters **a**, **e**, **i**, **o** and **u**.

Consonants are the letters of the alphabet which are <u>not</u> vowels.

What's next?

Use the words in the puzzles you have done to complete these activities.

Activity	Puzzle title	Date
Practise your handwriting. Write each phoneme or word five times in your book.		
Practise writing the words and then draw a picture for each one.		
Find three more words that begin with the same phoneme. For example, *cap, cat* and *cut* all begin with **c**.		
Find three more words that begin with the same blend of phonemes. For example, *flag, flip* and *flop* all begin with **fl**.		
Find five more words that end with the same phoneme. For example, *cat, hit, but, wet* and *net* all end with **t**.		
Find three more words that end with the same blend of phonemes. For example, *fast, fist* and *post* all end with **st**.		
Find three more words that rhyme.		
Put the words into sentences. Remember to start with a capital letter and end with a full stop!		

Words with S

Say the phoneme **s**. Now blend the phonemes to read the words below. Cut out the words that start with **s**. Stick them around the **s**un.

sad		cat	
six	6	sit	
net		pig	
dog		sun	

Words with t

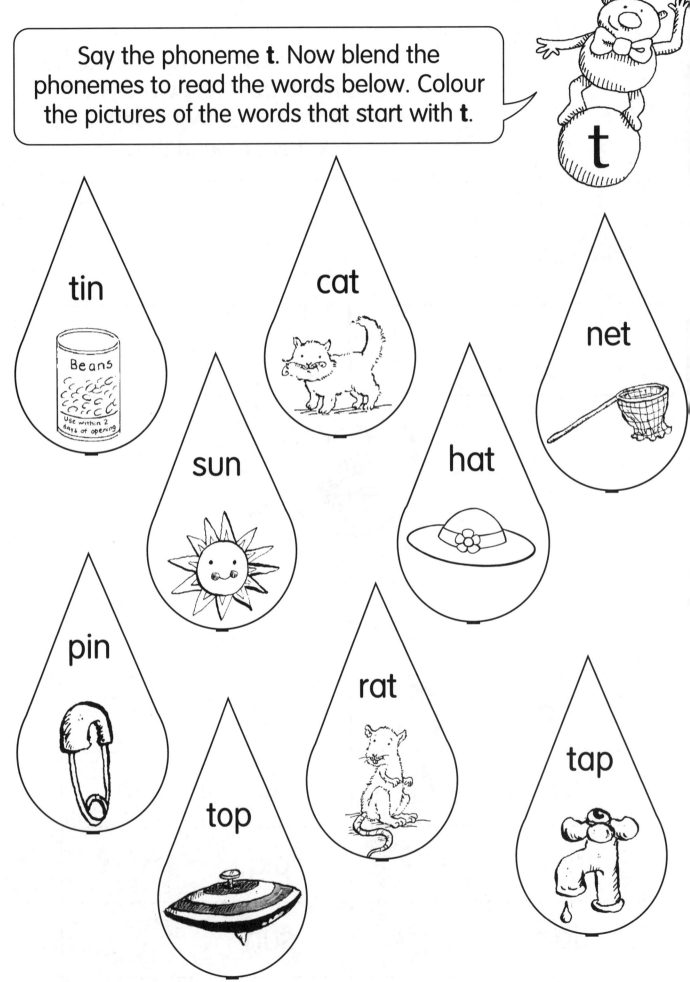

Say the phoneme **t**. Now blend the phonemes to read the words below. Colour the pictures of the words that start with **t**.

tin

cat

net

sun

hat

pin

rat

top

tap

6

Words with p

Say the phoneme **p**. Now blend the phonemes to read the words below. Colour the pictures of the words that start with **p**.

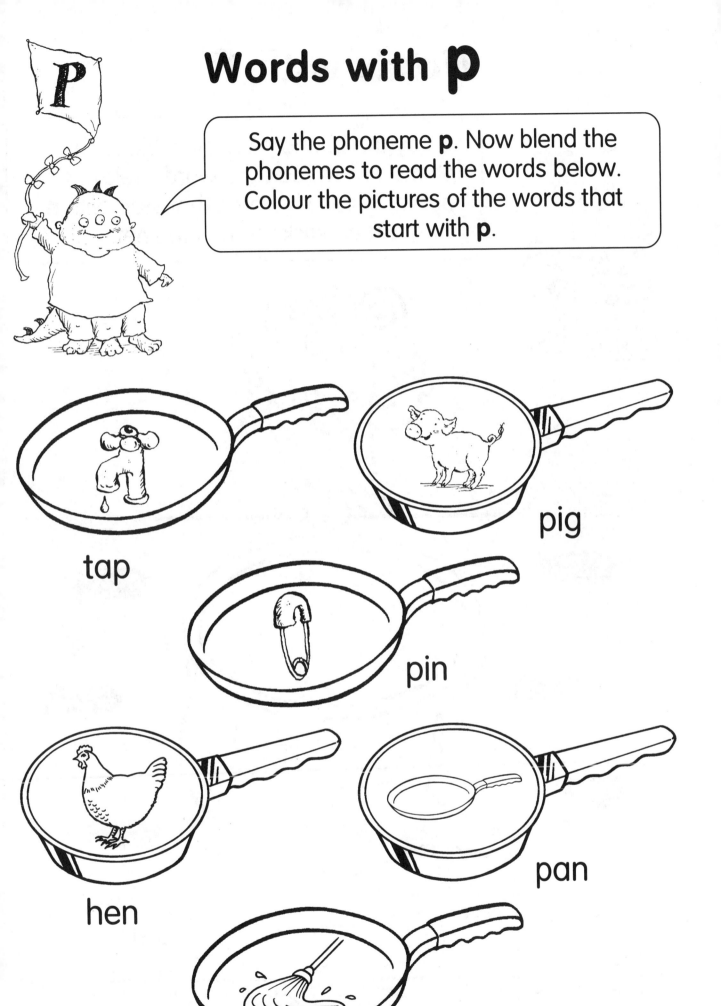

tap

pig

pin

hen

pan

mop

7

Words with **n**

Say the phoneme **n**. Now blend the phonemes to read the words below. Cut out the fish with words that start with **n**. Then stick them in the **n**et.

| nut | cap | pen |
| net | nun | man |

Words that begin with
n, p, s or t

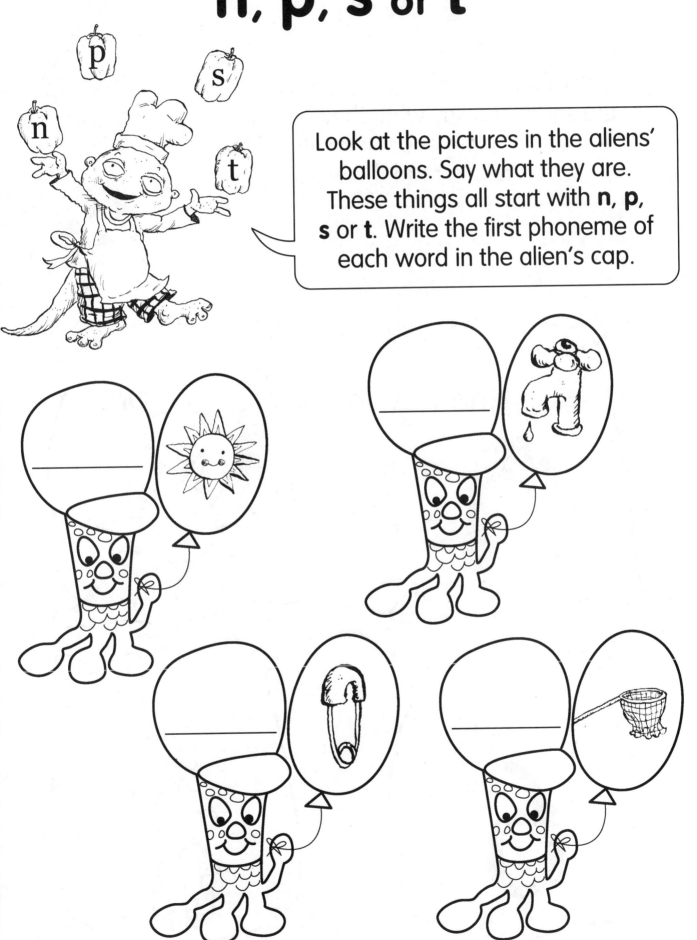

Look at the pictures in the aliens' balloons. Say what they are. These things all start with **n**, **p**, **s** or **t**. Write the first phoneme of each word in the alien's cap.

Words that begin with S

Say the phoneme **s**. Look at the pictures in the **s**acks and say what they are. Then write **s** to complete each word. Blend the phonemes to read the words.

___ad

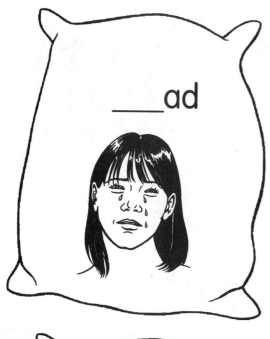

___un

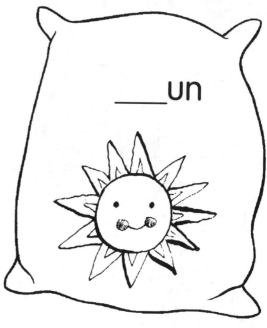

___ix

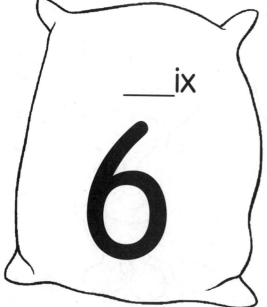

___it

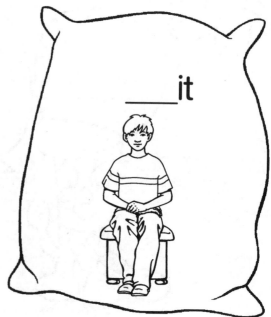

Words that begin with p

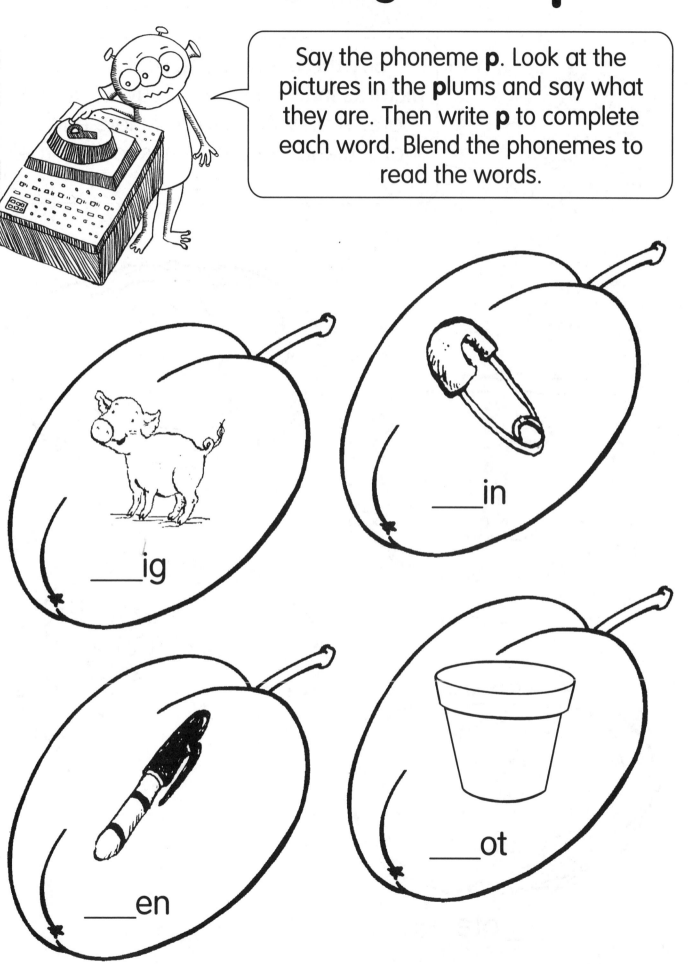

Say the phoneme **p**. Look at the pictures in the **p**lums and say what they are. Then write **p** to complete each word. Blend the phonemes to read the words.

___ig

___in

___en

___ot

Words that begin with n

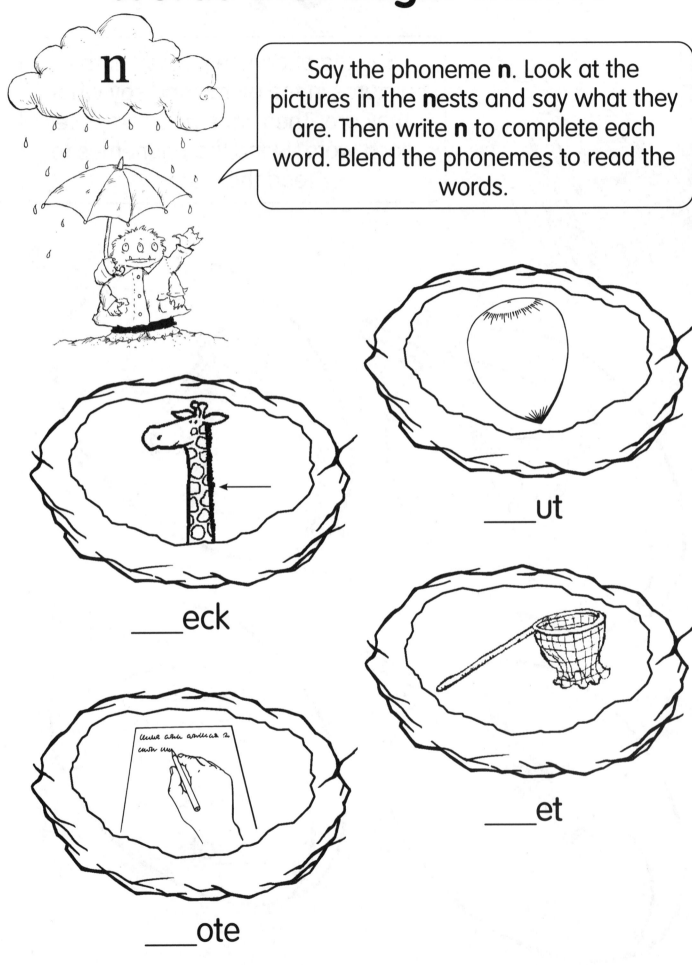

n

Say the phoneme **n**. Look at the pictures in the **n**ests and say what they are. Then write **n** to complete each word. Blend the phonemes to read the words.

___ut

___eck

___et

___ote

Words with C

Look at the pictures below and read the words. Join the words that start with **c** to the spaceship.

mop

cat

pot

tap

cap

car

mug

cot

cup

Words with h

Say the phoneme h. Colour the kites showing pictures that start with h. Cut out the hats and stick them on the aliens with h words to match the pictures.

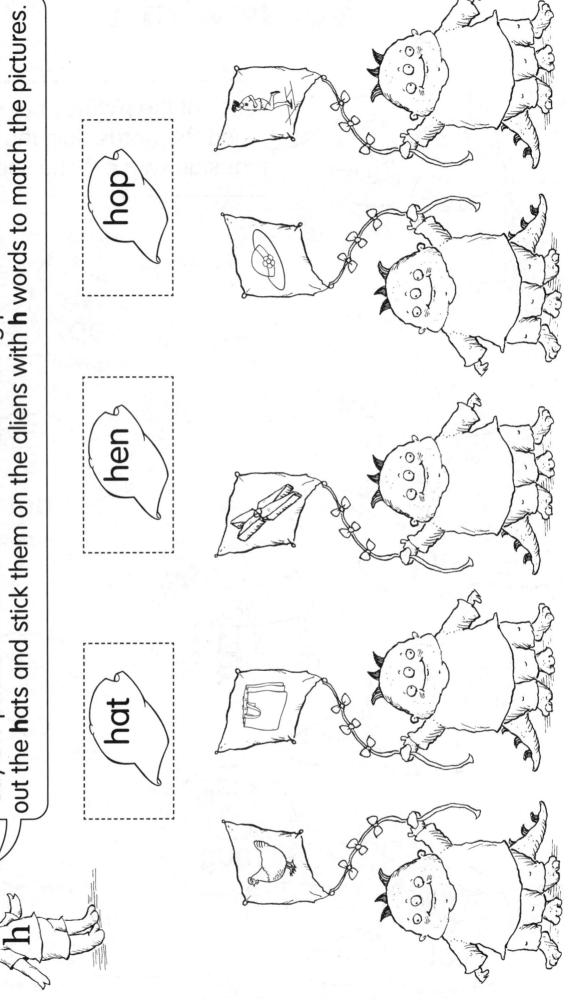

hop

hen

hat

h

Words with **r**

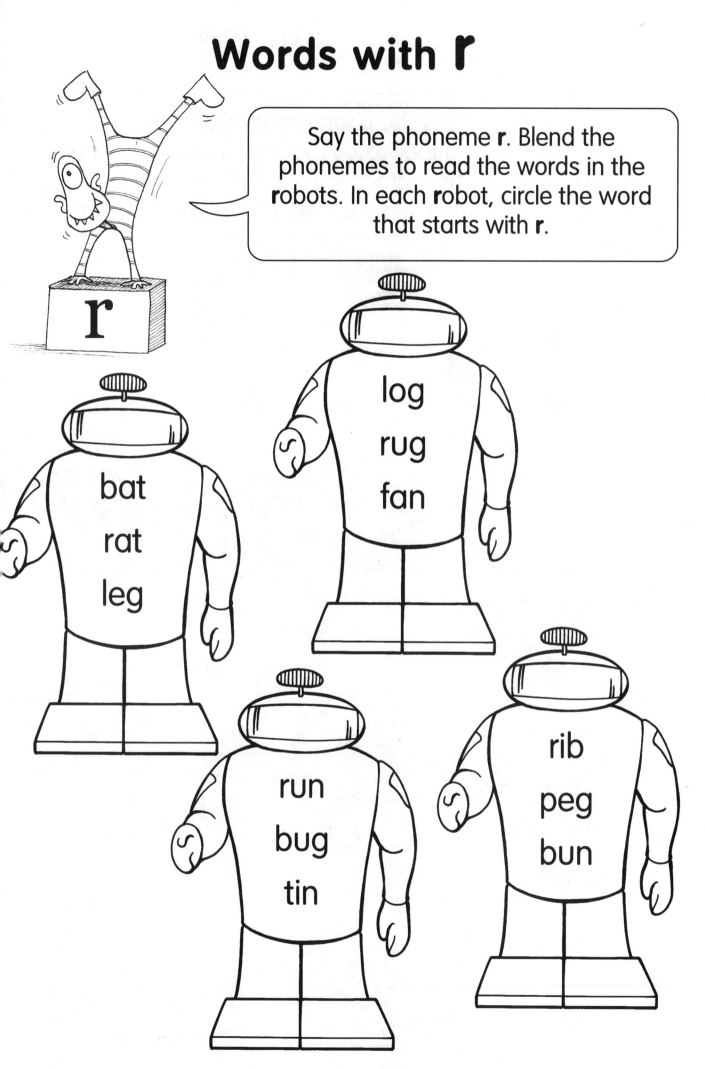

Say the phoneme **r**. Blend the phonemes to read the words in the **r**obots. In each **r**obot, circle the word that starts with **r**.

bat
rat
leg

log
rug
fan

run
bug
tin

rib
peg
bun

Words with m

Say the phoneme **m**. Colour the pictures of the words that begin with **m**. Blend the phonemes to read the words in the **mice**. Then join each **mouse** to the correct cheese.

mop

mat

mug

Words with **d**

Say the phoneme **d**. Blend the phonemes to read the words in the bones. Colour the bones with words that start with **d**. Then join the **d**og to the words that start with **d**.

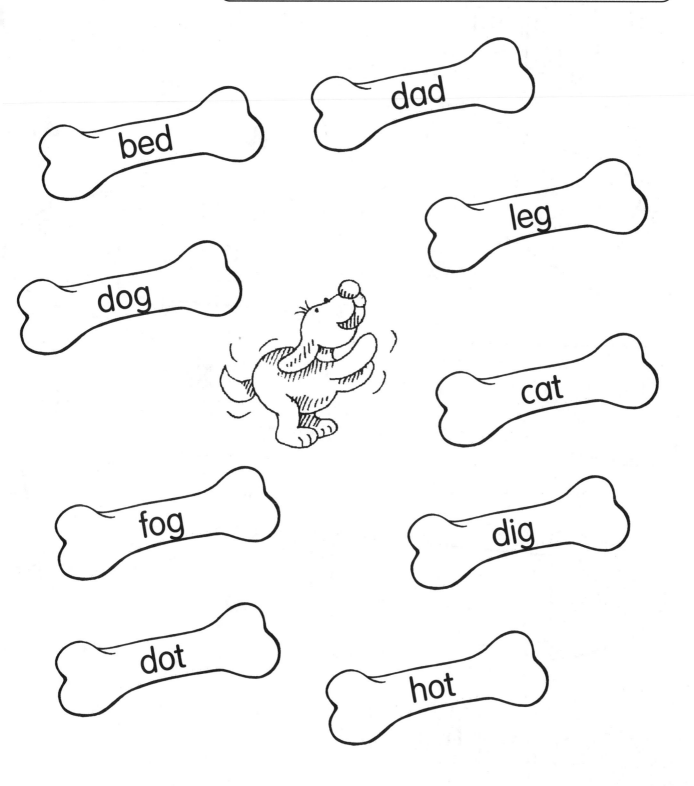

Words that begin with c, d, h, m or r

Look at the pictures and say what they are. Choose and cut out a phoneme to start each word. Then stick each one onto a rocket. Blend the phonemes to read the words.

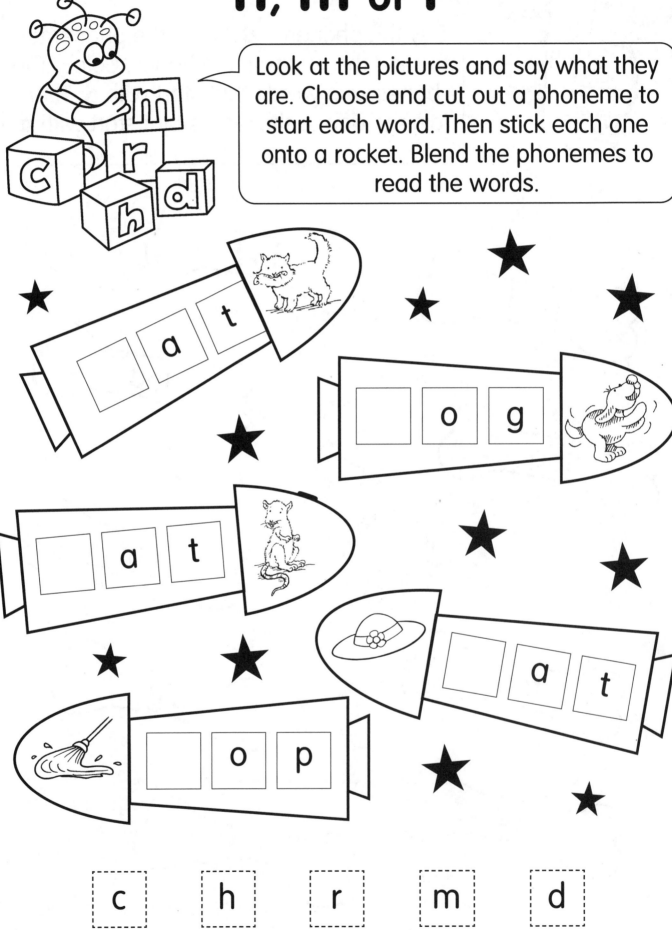

☐ a t

☐ o g

☐ a t

☐ a t

☐ o p

c   h   r   m   d

Words that begin with C

Look at the pictures in the **c**ups and say what they are. Write the missing **c** to complete each word. Join the words to the pictures.

___ut

___at

___ap

___ot

Words that begin with **h**

Say the phoneme **h**. Look at the pictures in the **h**ats and say what they are. Write the missing **h** to complete the words. Join the words to the pictures.

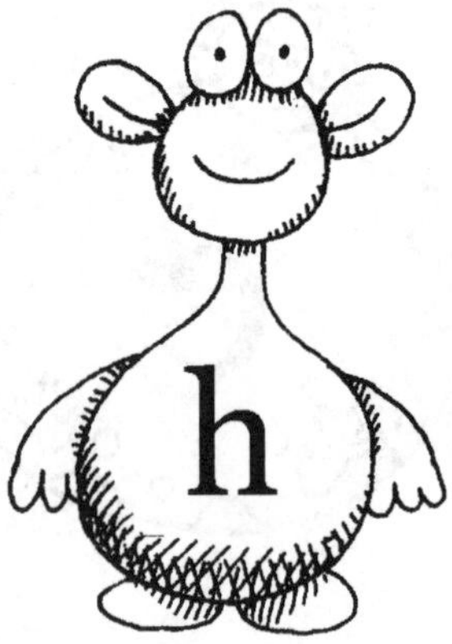

___at

___ot

___op

___en

20

Words that begin with **d**

Say the phoneme **d**. Look at the pictures in the **d**ishes and say what they are. Write the missing **d** to complete the words. Join the words to the pictures.

___ig

___ot

___ad

___og

Words with g

Say the phoneme **g**. Look at the pictures and say what they are. Colour the pictures of the words that begin with **g**.

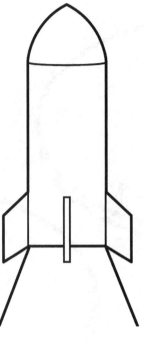

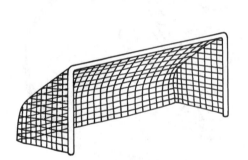

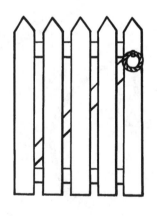

Words with l

log

bug

lip

bat

leg

cup

Words with **f**

Say the phoneme **f**. Look at the pictures and say what they are. Can you hear the phoneme they start with? Colour the pictures that start with **f**. Then join these pictures to the **f**rog.

Words with **b**

Say the phoneme **b.** Blend the phonemes to read the words. Look at the pictures in the **b**ells and then circle the word that starts with **b** under each one.

bat
hat
peg

mug
bug
cap

red
net
bed

bag
fog
rag

pin
bin
cot

bun
sun
leg

Words that begin with b, f, g and l

Say the phonemes b, f, g and l. Look at the pictures below. Three pictures on each planet start with the same phoneme. Colour these and then cross the odd one out.

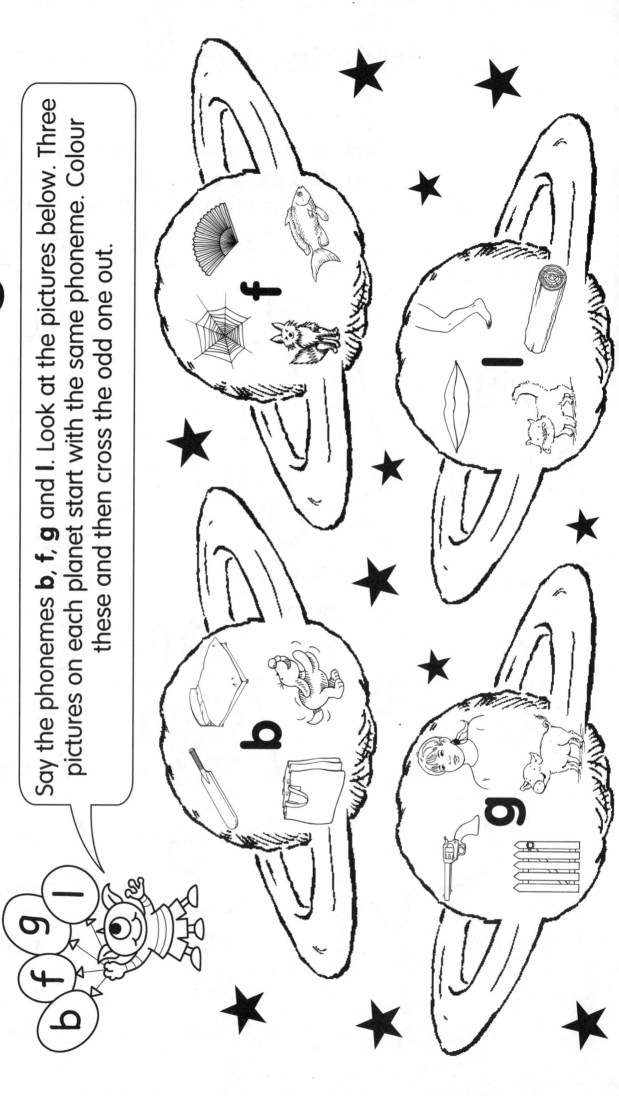

Words that begin with
b, f or l

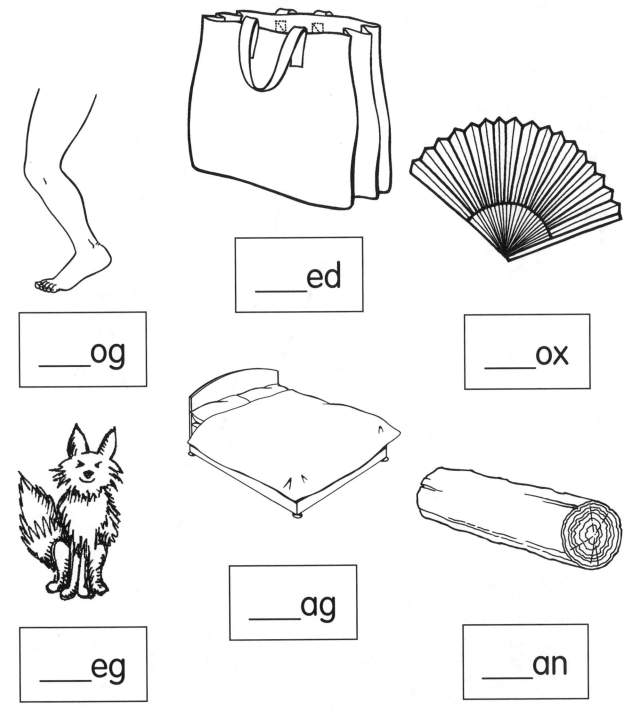

___ed

___og

___ox

___ag

___eg

___an

Words that begin with b

Look at the pictures below and say what they are. Say the phonemes in the torch light. The big phoneme on the torch is the one at the start of the word. Use the big phoneme, a middle phoneme and a phoneme at the end to make your words. Write them on the lines next to the pictures and then blend the phonemes to read the words.

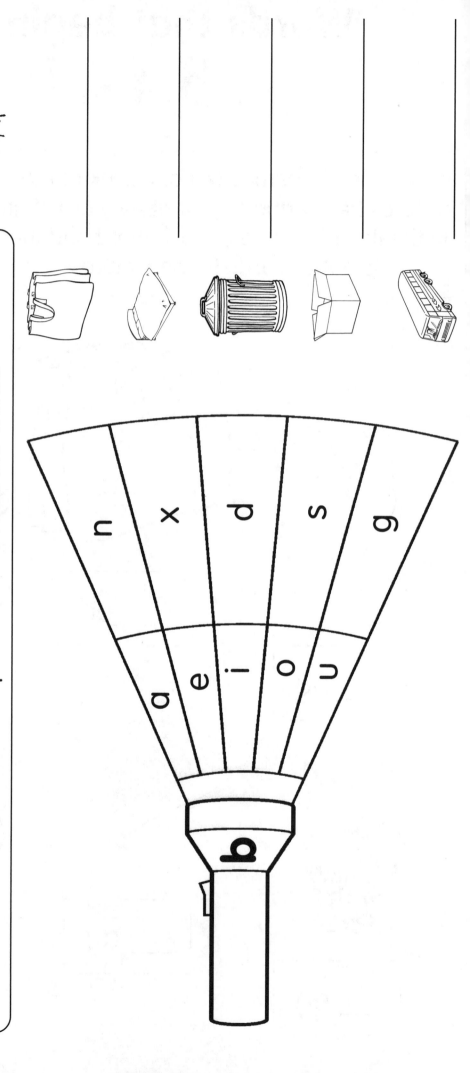

Words that begin with C

Look at the pictures below and say what they are. Say the phonemes in the torch light. The big phoneme on the torch is the one at the start of the word. Use the big phoneme, a middle phoneme and a phoneme at the end to make your words. Write them on the lines next to the pictures and then blend the phonemes to read the words.

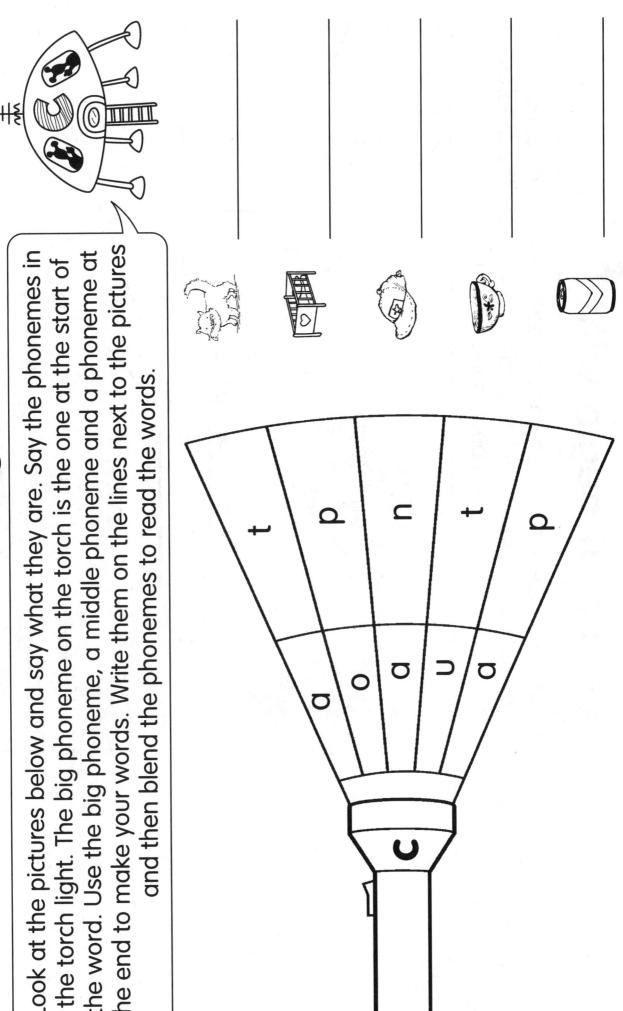

29

Words that begin with f

Look at the words and blend the phonemes to read them. Then cut out the phonemes and stick them on the rocket to spell the words in the pictures. An example has been done for you.

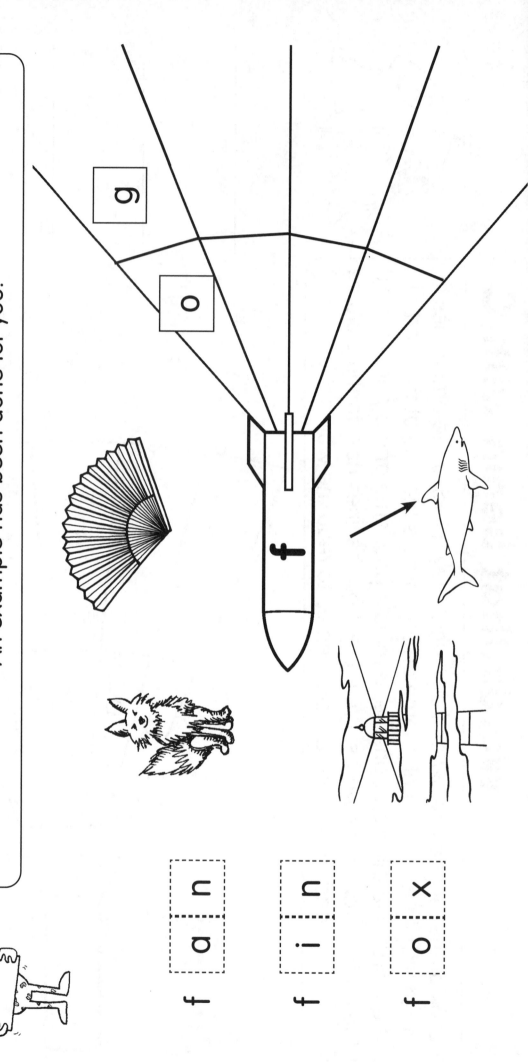

g

o

f a n
f

f i n
f

f o x
f

Words that begin with h

Blend the phonemes to read the words. Then cut out the letters and stick them on the star picture to spell the words.

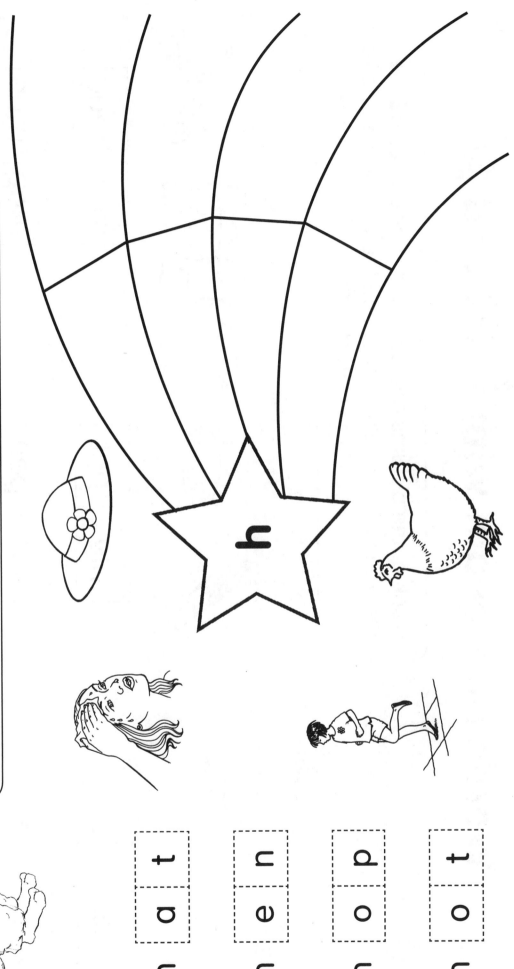

h	a	t
h	e	n
h	o	p
h	o	t

Words that begin with l, m and p

Look at the pictures and say what they are. Blend the phonemes to read the words and then join each one to the correct picture.

mug   man

mop   map

pot   pig

pen   pan

leg   lip

log   lap

Words that begin with **r, s** and **t**

Join the phonemes together and write the words on the lines. Then join the words to the pictures.

r	u	n	_____
r	i	b	_____
r	u	g	_____

s	a	d	_____
s	u	n	_____
s	i	x	_____

t	o	p	_____
t	a	p	_____
t	i	n	_____

First phonemes

Choose a phoneme to complete each word. You can use some phonemes more than once.

p s t b d c n l

Example:  $\underline{r}$ug

 ___at

 ___og

 ___un

___en

 ___ed

___ap

___et

___ap

___ag

 ___eg

First phonemes

Choose a phoneme from a star to complete each word. Then join the words to a picture.

☆ z _r_ at

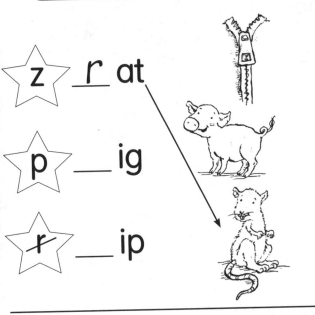

☆ p __ ig

☆ r __ ip

☆ b __ en

☆ m __ ox

☆ t __ ug

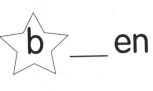

10

☆ p __ op

☆ r __ in

☆ t __ ib

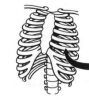

☆ b __ eg

☆ p __ up

☆ c __ at

☆ b __ an

☆ l __ ug

☆ p __ og

What are the first phonemes?

Say the phonemes in the planets. Blend the phonemes to read the words in the stars. Then join the words to their first phonemes.

w

b

t

m

bed   ten   man

d

s

web   dad   sun

k

kit   hat

f

rat   net   fox

r

h

pin   leg   jug

p

j

n

l

Words with a

Say the phoneme **a**. Look at the pictures in the flags and write the middle phoneme **a** for each word. Blend the phonemes to read the words.

t___p

b___g

h___t

b___t

c___t

m___n

37

Words with i

Say the phoneme **i**. Blend the phonemes to read the words. Cut out the ones with the middle phoneme **i** and stick them in the bin.

pin

tin

mop

pen

lid

cup

Words with a or i

Say the phonemes **a** and **i**. Write **a** or **i** to complete the words. Blend the phonemes to read the words.

p___n

f___n

b___g

a or i

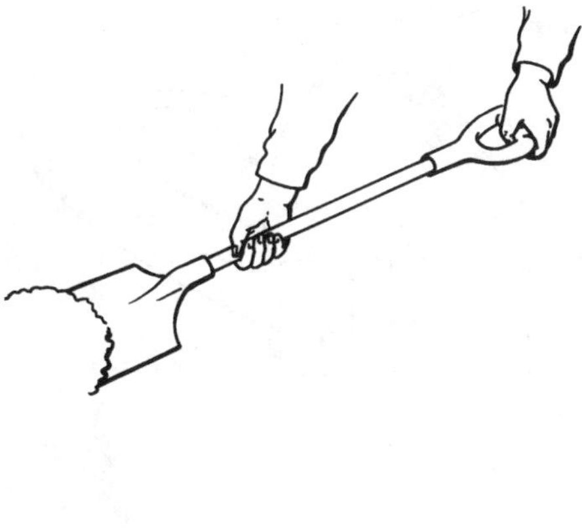

d___g

t___n

c___t

Words with e

Say the phoneme **e**. Look at the pictures and say what they are. Cut out each phoneme **e** and stick it to complete the words. Then colour the middle phoneme **e**.

| n | | t |

| l | | g |

| h | | n |

| b | | d |

| p | | n |

e   e   e   e   e

Words with **a** or **e**

Say the phonemes **a** and **e**. Blend the phonemes to read the words. Circle the word that matches each picture. Some of the words are nonsense words.

leg

lag

ret

rat

het

hat

nat

net

pan

pen

pag

peg

Words with e or i

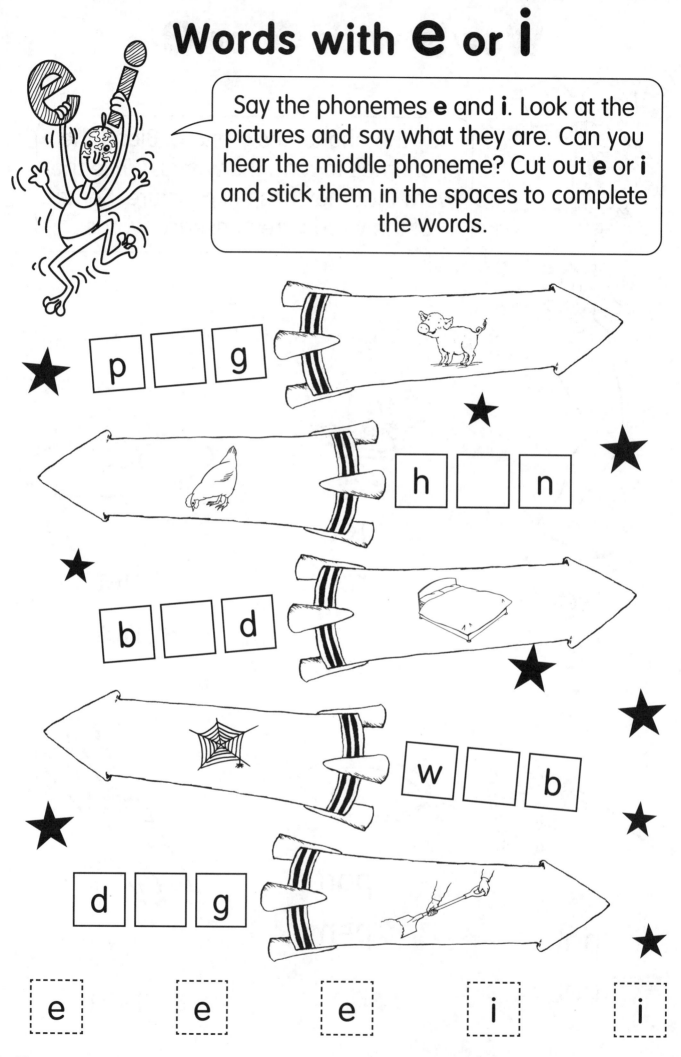

Say the phonemes **e** and **i**. Look at the pictures and say what they are. Can you hear the middle phoneme? Cut out **e** or **i** and stick them in the spaces to complete the words.

p ☐ g

h ☐ n

b ☐ d

w ☐ b

d ☐ g

e   e   e   i   i

Words with O

Say the phoneme **o**. Look at the pictures and say what they are. Read the words in the bricks. Colour the bricks with a middle phoneme **o**. Join the pictures to the words with an **o**.

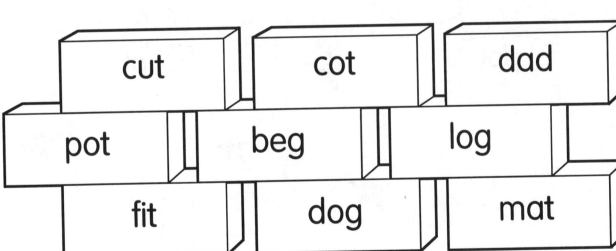

cut

cot

dad

pot

beg

log

fit

dog

mat

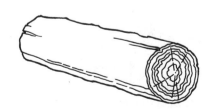

Words with **i** or **o**

i or o

Say the phonemes **i** and **o**. Look at the pictures below. Blend the phonemes to read the words. Then join the pictures to the words.

pit

pot

hit

hot

tip

top

dig

dog

44

Words with O or U

Say the phonemes **o** and **u**. Look at the pictures below and say what they are. Cut out the pictures and words. Stick those with **u** in the c**u**p and those with **o** in the b**o**x.

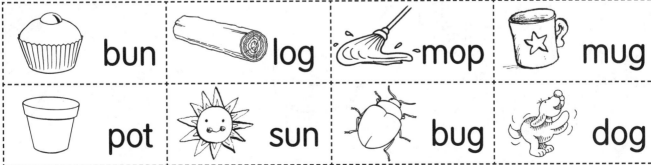

bun log mop mug

pot sun bug dog

Vowel phonemes

Say the phonemes **a**, **e**, **i**, **o** and **u**. Blend the phonemes to read the words. Can you hear the middle phonemes? Join each word to a volcano that matches the middle phoneme.

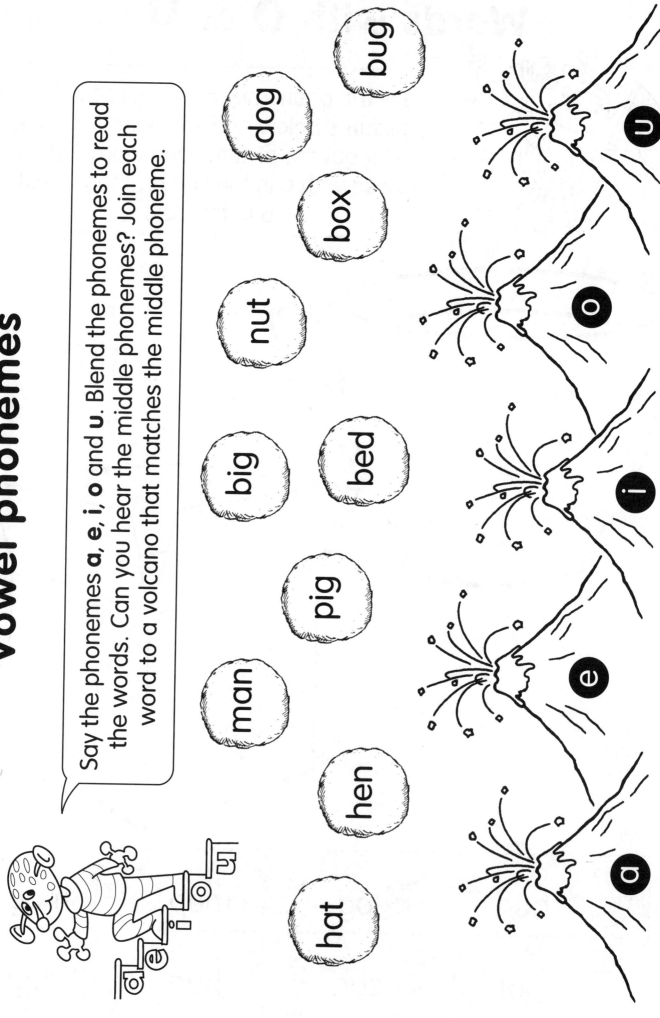

dog

bug

box

nut

big

bed

pig

man

hen

hat

u

o

i

e

a

Middle phonemes

Say the phonemes **a** and **e**. Write the middle phonemes in the words and then blend the phonemes to read the words. Join the words to the pictures.

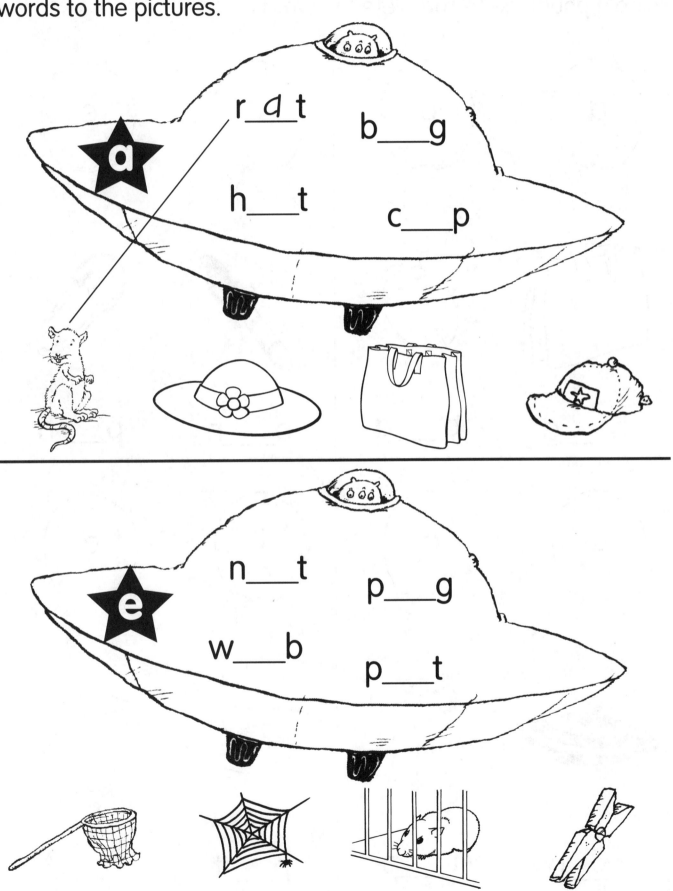

r_a_t   b___g

h___t   c___p

a

n___t   p___g

w___b   p___t

e

Middle vowel phonemes

Say the phonemes **a**, **e**, **i**, **o** and **u**. Look at the pictures and say what they are. Can you hear the middle phonemes? Write the middle phoneme to complete the words.

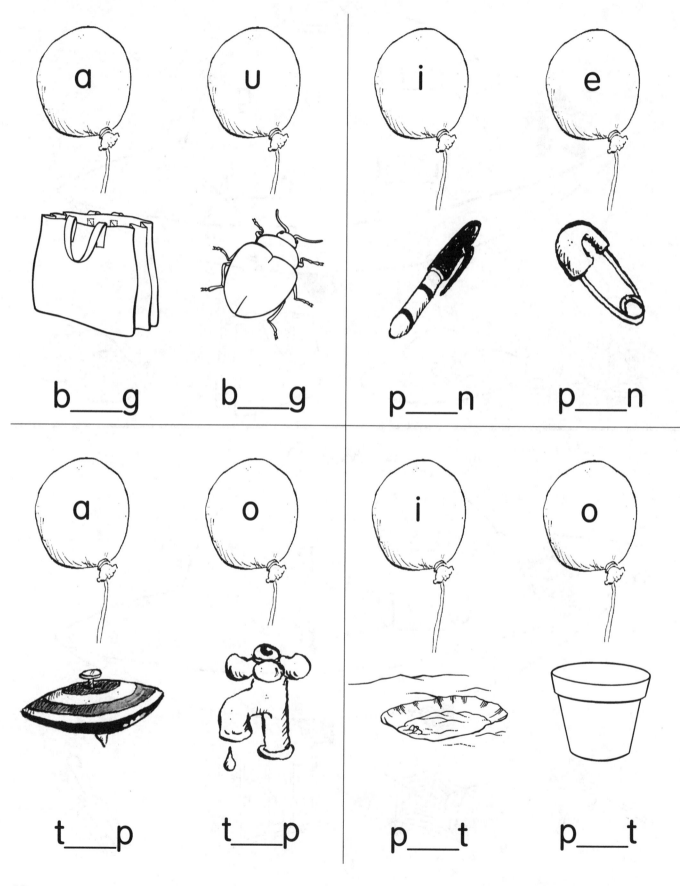

b___g   b___g   p___n   p___n

t___p   t___p   p___t   p___t

Middle vowel phonemes

Look at the pictures and say what they are. Choose a middle phoneme to complete each word and then blend the phonemes to read the words.

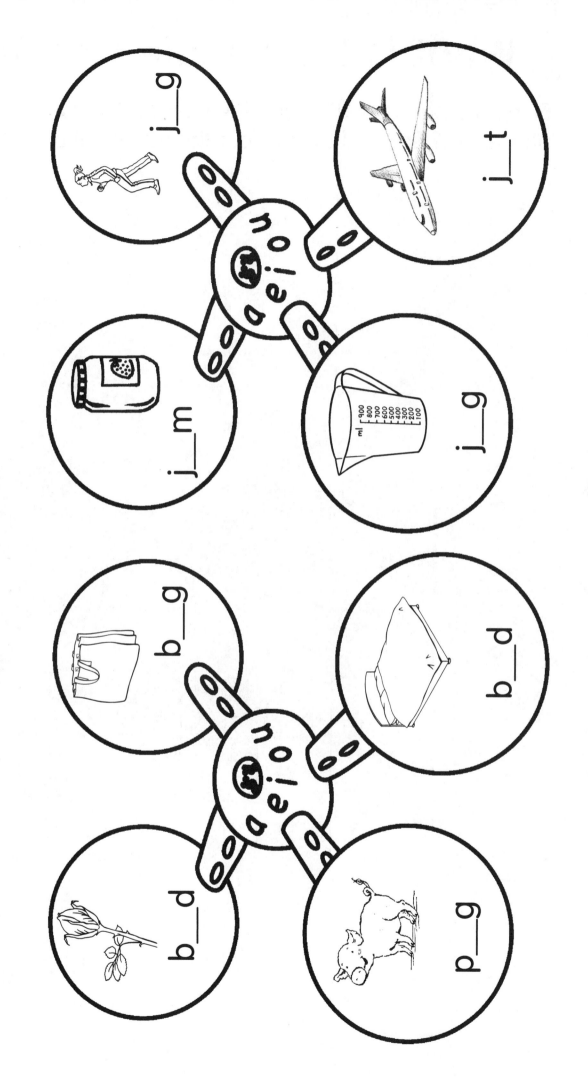

What is the middle phoneme?

Blend the phonemes to read the words. Can you hear the middle phonemes? Say and then colour the middle phonemes.

cap dog

mop web

pig bug

map

tin

nut net

Words that end in **t**

Say the phoneme **t**. Look at the pictures in the ping-pong ba**t**s and say what they are. They all end with **t**. Write **t** at the end of each word and then blend the phonemes to read the words.

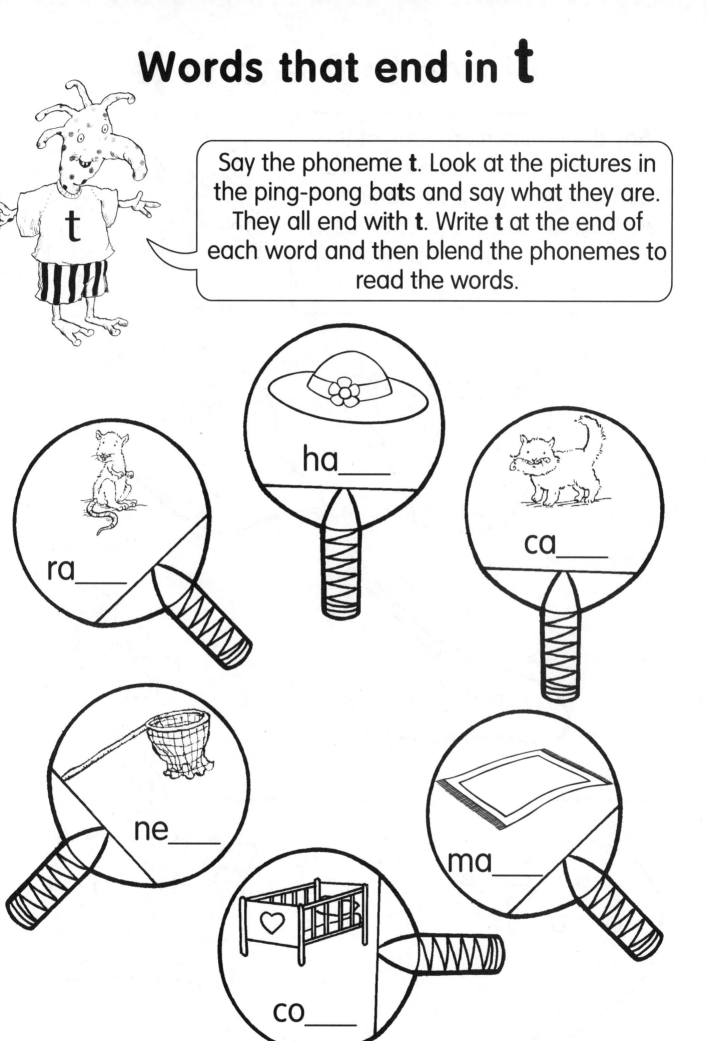

ra____

ha____

ca____

ne____

ma____

co____

Words that end in **p**

Say the phoneme **p**. Look at the pictures and say what they are. Can you hear the **p** at the end of each word? Use the phonemes in the pictures to write each word. All the words end in **p**.

p u c

p c a

___ ___ ___

___ ___ ___

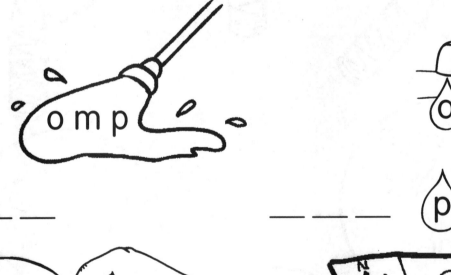

o m p

a

t

p

___ ___ ___ ___

___ ___ ___

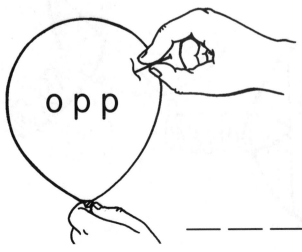

o p p

m p

a

___ ___ ___ ___

___ ___ ___

Words that end in n

Say the phoneme n. Look at the pictures in the planets and say what they are. Can you hear the n at the end of the word? Blend the phonemes to read the words. Then cut out the words and stick them under the pictures.

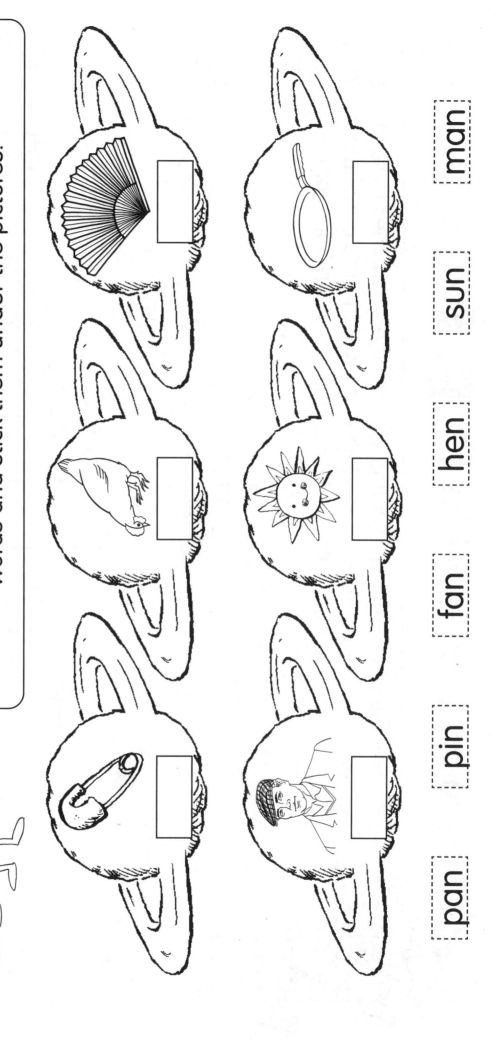

| pan | pin | fan | hen | sun | man |

Words that end in **n, p, s and t**

Say the phonemes **n**, **p**, **s** and **t**. Blend the phonemes to read the words on the shooting stars. Join each word to the phoneme in the planet to match its last letter. One has been done for you.

hen

tap

cap

bus

nut

pen

cat

s   n   p

t

Words that end in ck

ck sounds the same as the phoneme **k**. Look at the pictures in the socks below. Blend the phonemes to read the words. Circle **ck** in each word. Cut out the socks and stick them in pairs on a separate piece of paper, by matching each picture to a word.

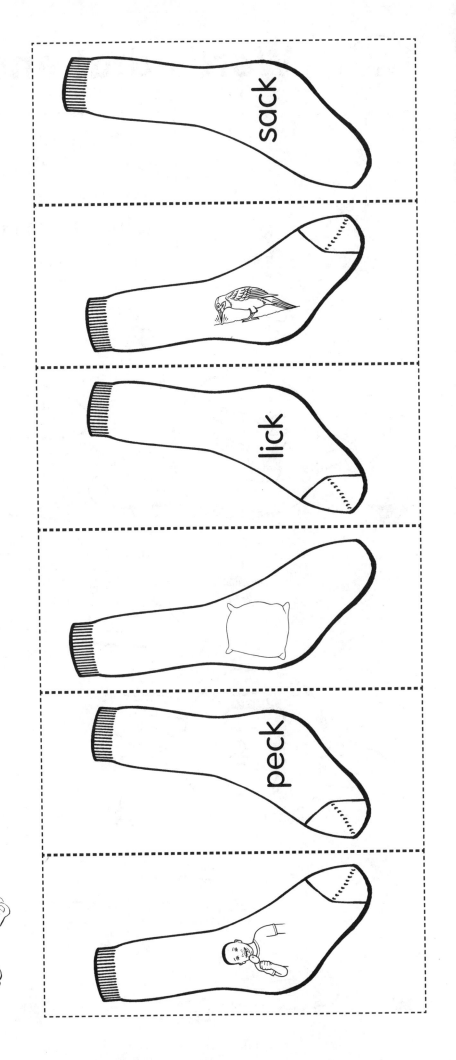

sack

lick

peck

Words that end in m

Say the phoneme **m**. Look at the pictures in the planets and say what they are. Can you hear the phoneme at the end of each word? Colour the pictures of words that end in **m**.

Words that end in **d**

Say the phoneme **d**. Blend the phonemes to read the words below. Can you hear the phoneme at the end of each word? Circle the words that end in **d** and join them to the **d** in the middle planet.

Words that end in **ck**, **d** and **m**

Look at the pictures and say what they are. Write the missing phonemes at the end of each word.

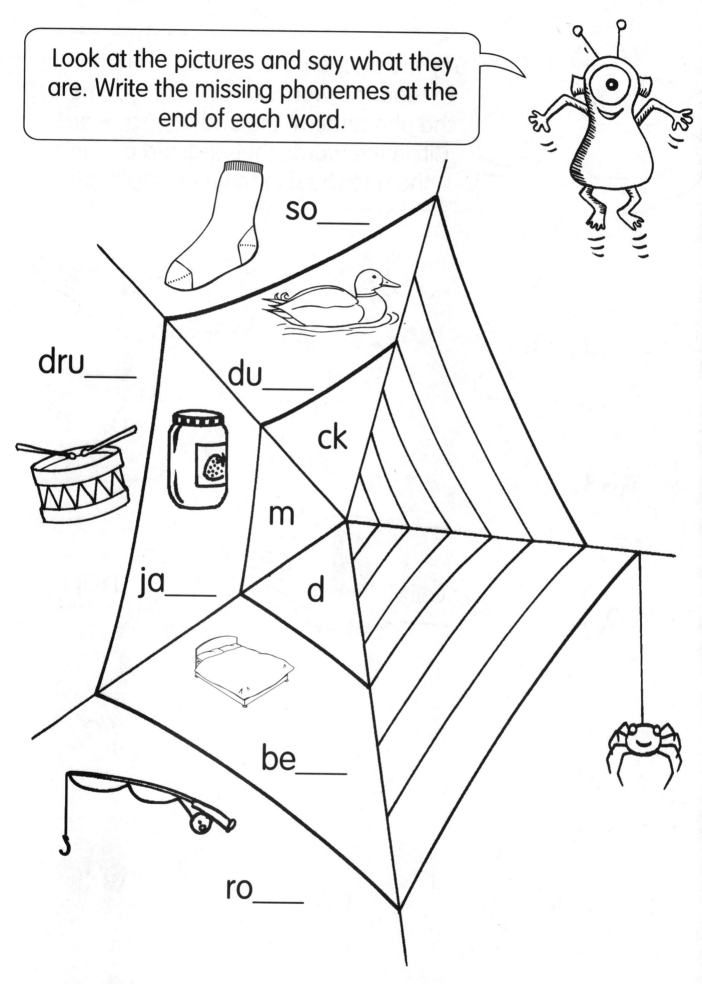

so____

dru____

du____

ck

m

ja____

d

be____

ro____

Words that end in g

Say the phoneme **g**. Look at the pictures and say what they are. Can you hear the phoneme at the end of each word? Write the final phonemes and colour the pictures of the words that end in **g**.

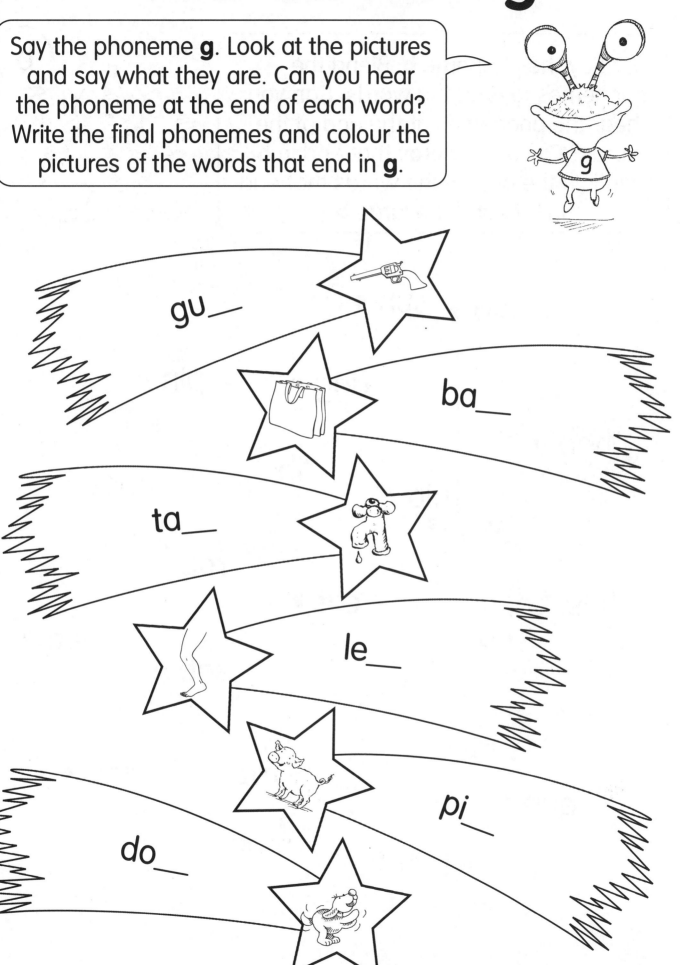

gu__

ba__

ta__

le__

pi__

do__

59

Words that end in **b**

Say the phoneme **b**. Blend the phonemes to read the words. Can you hear the phonemes at the end of the words? Circle the words that end in **b**. Then join the dots of the words that end in **b** to find the large **b**.

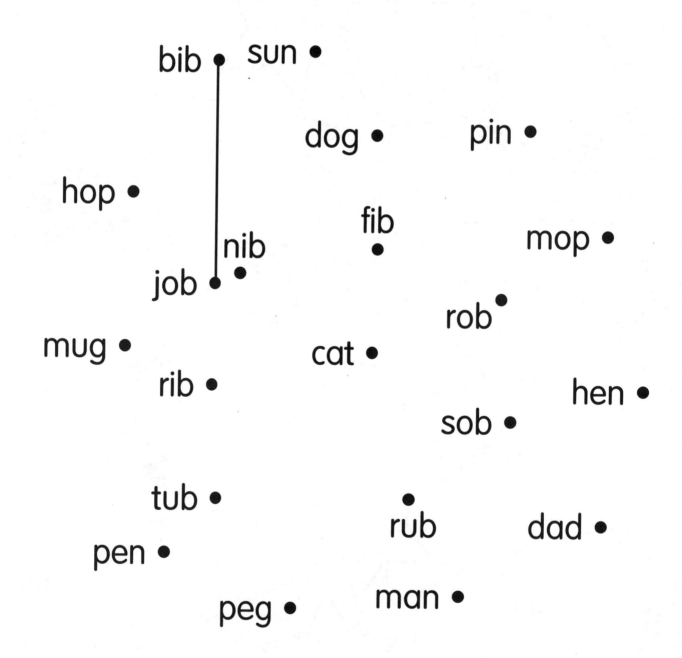

bib •   sun •

dog •   pin •

hop •

fib •

nib   mop •

job • •

rob •

mug •   cat •

rib •   hen •

sob •

tub •

rub   dad •

pen •

peg •   man •

Words that begin with **j**

Say the phoneme j. Look at the pictures and say what they are. Can you hear the phonemes at the start of these words? Cut out the things that begin with j and stick them in the jar.

jar

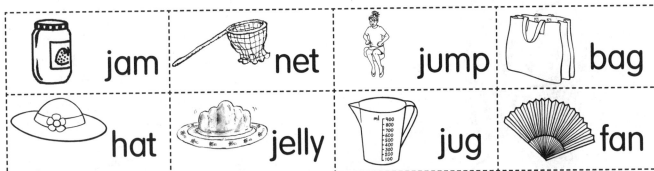

jam   net   jump   bag

hat   jelly   jug   fan

Words with **W** and **Z**

Say the phonemes **w** and **z**. Look at the pictures and say what they are. Can you hear the phonemes at the start of the words? Join each balloon to an alien with that phoneme.

Words that begin with
j, w or z

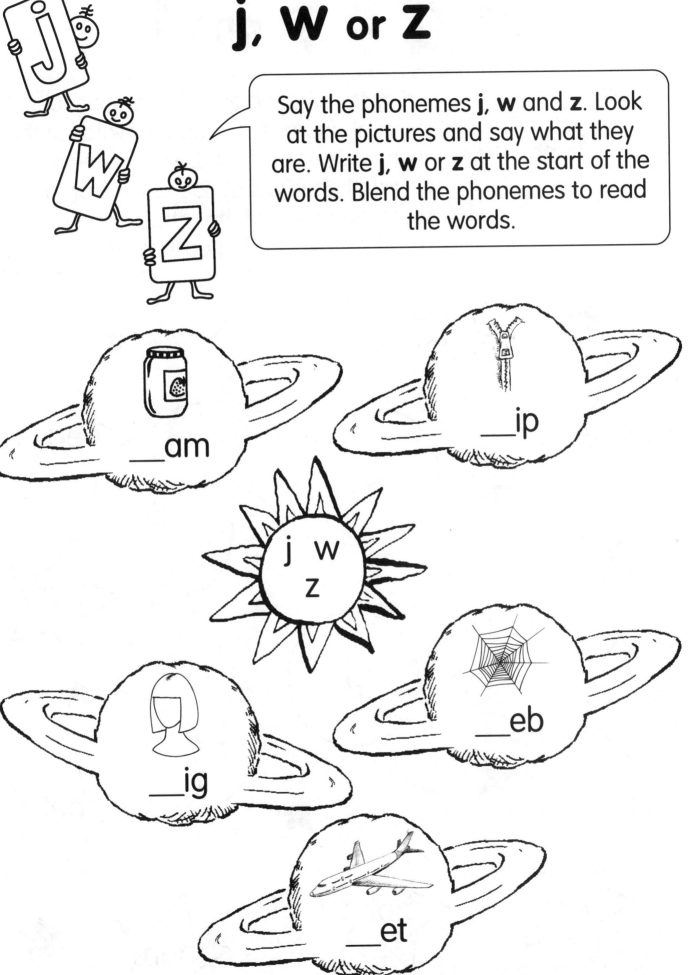

Say the phonemes **j**, **w** and **z**. Look at the pictures and say what they are. Write **j**, **w** or **z** at the start of the words. Blend the phonemes to read the words.

__am

__ip

j w z

__ig

__eb

__et

Words that end in
d, g, n, p and t

Say the phonemes in the moons. Blend the phonemes to read the words in the stars. Can you hear the phoneme at the end of each word? Join each star to the moon that matches the phoneme at the end of each word.

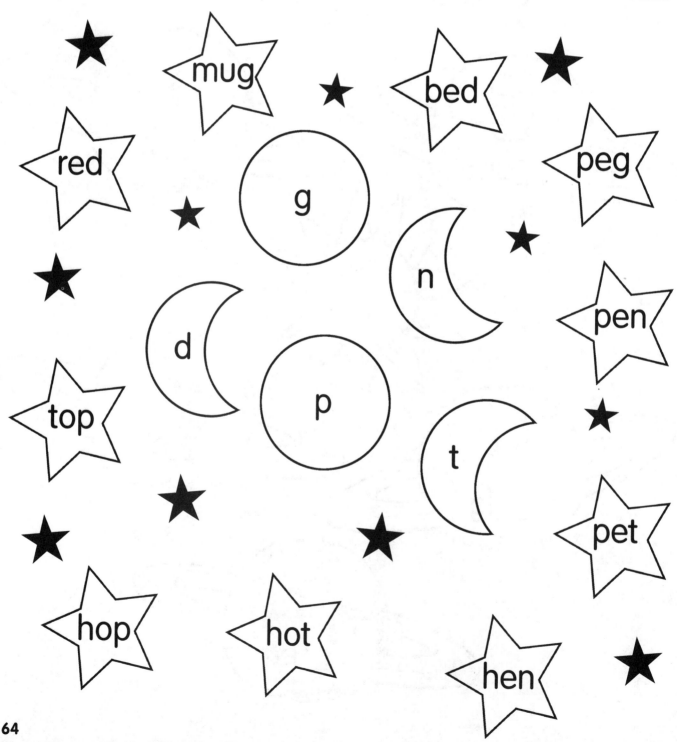

Words that end in g and n

Say the phonemes g and n. Look at the pictures and say what they are. Can you hear the phonemes at the end of the words? Cut out the pictures and stick those with the same final phoneme in either the sun or the jug.

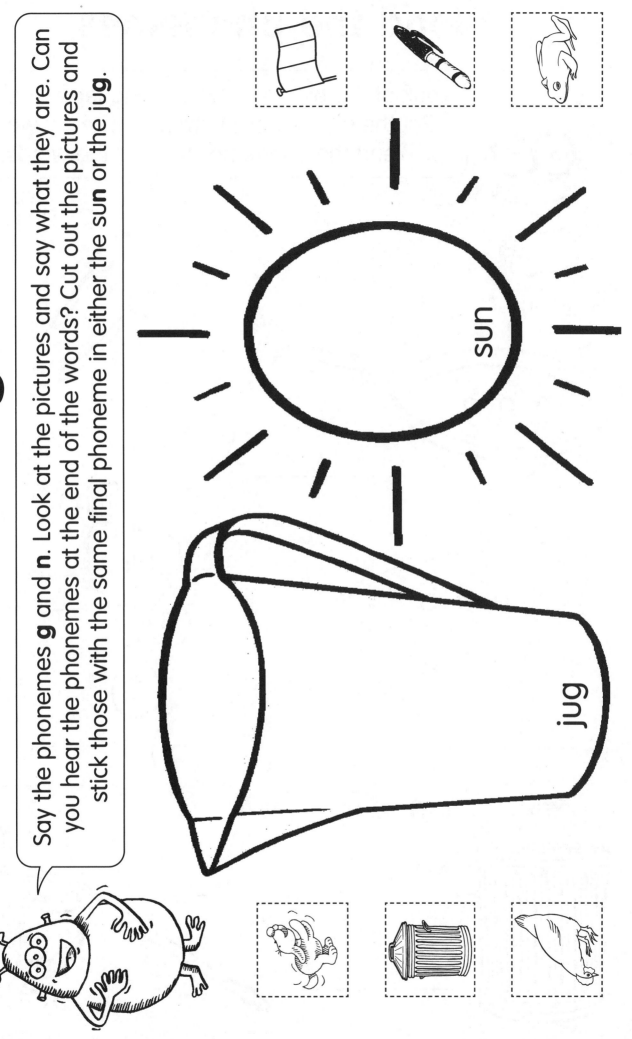

sun

jug

Blend the phonemes

Look at the pictures and the phonemes below.
Put the phonemes in order to make a word.
Blend the phonemes to read the words.

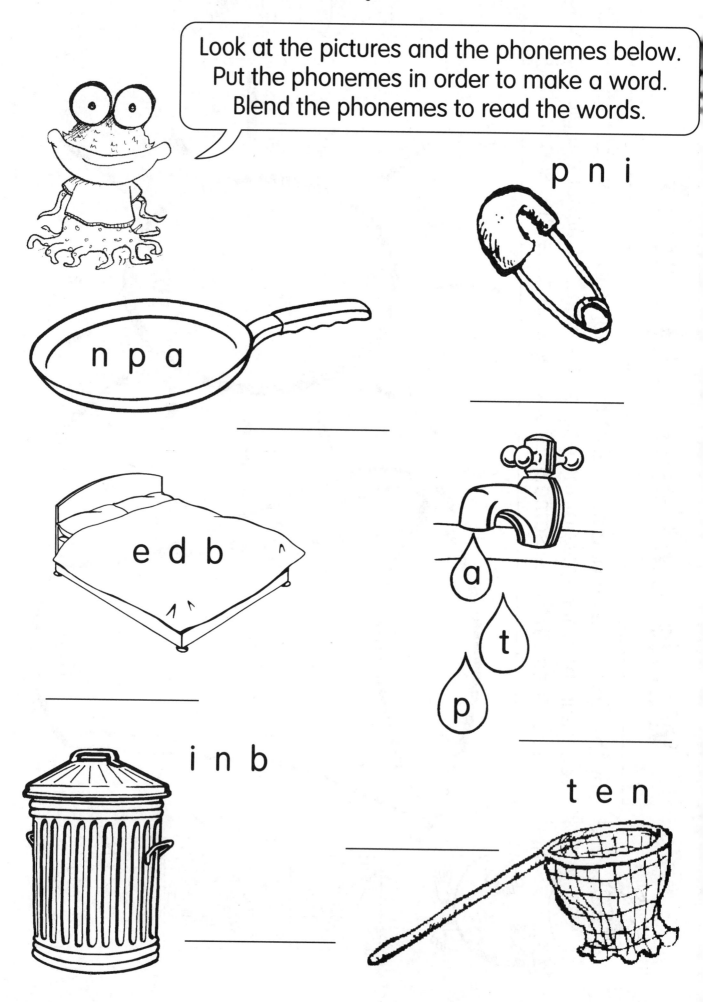

p n i

n p a

e d b

a

t

p

i n b

t e n

The ai phoneme

Look at the pictures below and say what they are. Can you hear the phoneme **ai** in the middle? Can you hear the phonemes at the start and at the end of the words? Cut out the phonemes below and stick them in the spaces to complete the words. Blend the phonemes to read the words.

| | a i | |

| | a i | |

| | a i | |

| | a i | |

| | a i | |

| l | s | n | l | j | t | l | r | l | n |

The **oa** phoneme

oa

Look at the pictures below and say what they are. Blend the phonemes to read the words. Can you hear the phoneme **oa**? Circle the correct word for each picture.

boat   road   soap

toad   soap   goat

toad   goat   coat

road   toad   boat

goat   soap   coat

coat   boat   road

The **igh** phoneme spelt **ie**

Blend the phonemes to read the words in the boxes below. Can you hear the **igh** phoneme? It is sometimes spelt **ie**. Look at the pictures and read the sentences. Cut out the **ie** words and stick them in the gaps.

1. Apple [　　] is nice

2. My dad wears a [　　] .

3. It is bad to [　　] .

4. I like meat [　　] and chips.

5. I [　　] down on my bed.

6. I can [　　] my laces.

```
tie    pie    lie    tie    spiel    lie
```

The **ee** phoneme

Look at the pictures below and say what they are. Can you hear the phoneme **ee**? Join the phonemes together to make the words. Write the words on the lines. Blend the phonemes to read the words.

| b | ee | _____ |

| sh | ee p | _____ |

3

| th r | ee | _____ |

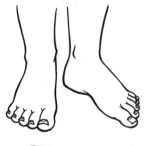

| f | ee t | _____ |

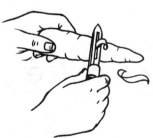

| p | ee l | _____ |

The **or** phoneme

Blend the phonemes to read the words. Can you hear the **or** phoneme? It can also be spelt **oor** and **our**. Look at the pictures and say what they are. Colour the correct picture for each word.

door

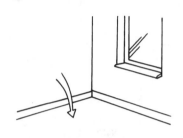 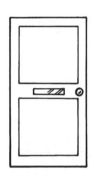 

★ ★

floor

  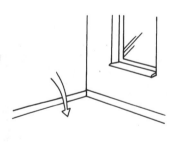

★ ★

four

 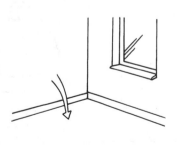 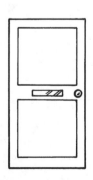

★ ★

Words that end in ng

Look at the pictures and say what they are. The words all end with the phoneme **ng**. Write the missing phoneme to complete the words. Then blend the phonemes to read the words.

r i ☐

h a ☐

s o ☐

f a ☐

k i ☐

w i ☐

d i ☐   d o ☐

Words that begin with V

Can you say the phoneme **v**? Blend the phonemes to read the words below. Look at the pictures in the **v**olcanoes. Then cut out the words and stick each one under the correct picture.

| v | e | t |

| v | e | s | t |

| v | a | n |

The short OO phoneme

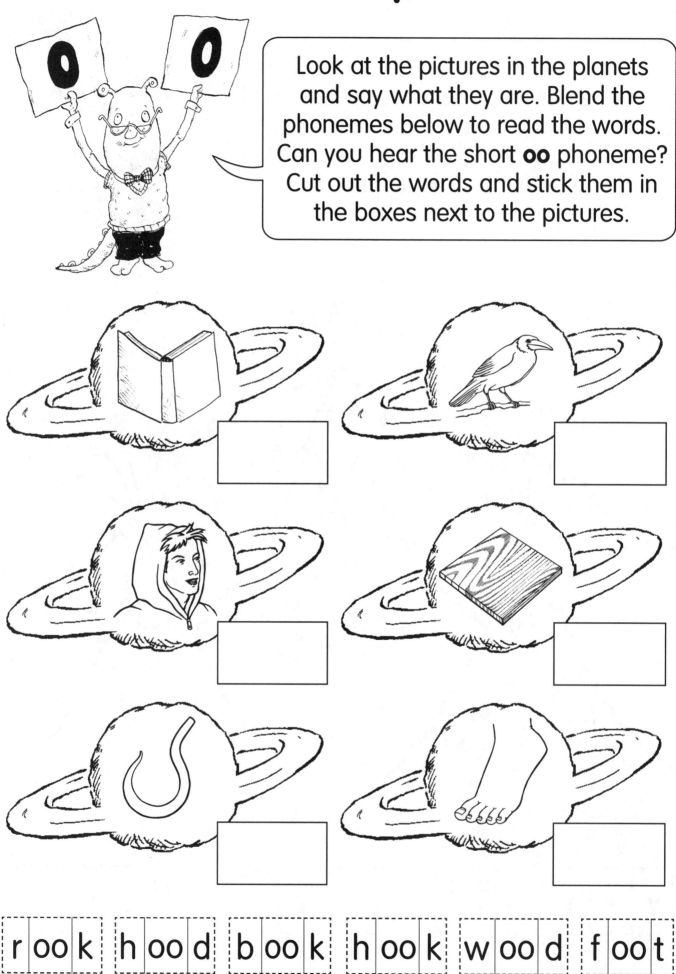

Look at the pictures in the planets and say what they are. Blend the phonemes below to read the words. Can you hear the short **oo** phoneme? Cut out the words and stick them in the boxes next to the pictures.

| r | oo | k | h | oo | d | b | oo | k | h | oo | k | w | oo | d | f | oo | t |

The long OO phoneme

Look at the pictures and say what they are. Can you hear the long **oo** phoneme? Cut out the phonemes at the bottom of the page and stick them in the empty boxes to spell the words.

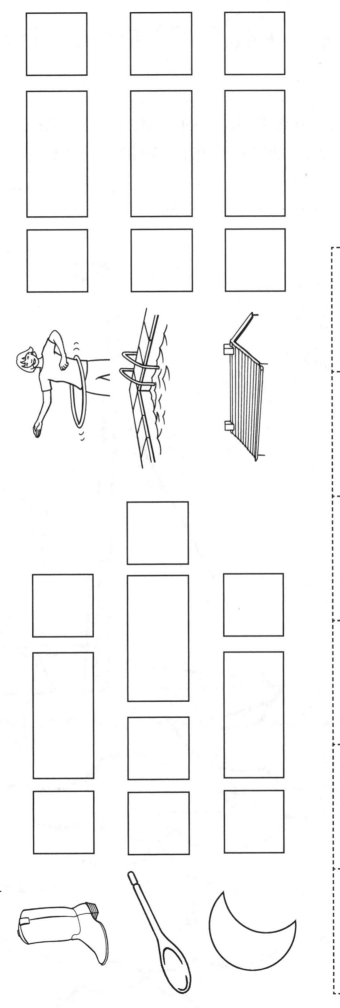

oo	oo	oo	oo	oo	oo
b	n	l	m	h	p
n	l	m	h	p	r
f	p	s	t	s	t
p				p	s
				n	p
				f	n
				p	f
					p

75

The **igh** phoneme spelt **y**

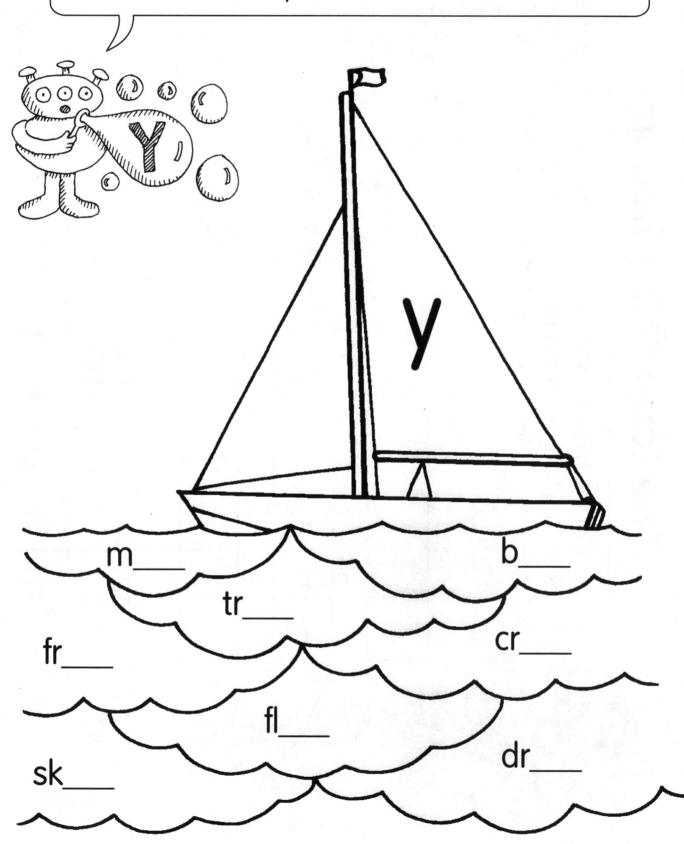

m____

b____

tr____

fr____

cr____

fl____

sk____

dr____

Words that end in X

Look at the rockets below. Write the missing **x** in each word and then blend the phonemes to read the words.

si ___

fo ___

bo ___

mi ___

Final phonemes

Look at the pictures below and say what they are. Can you hear the phoneme at the end of each word? Cut out the phonemes and stick them in the spaces to complete the words. Blend the phonemes to read the words.

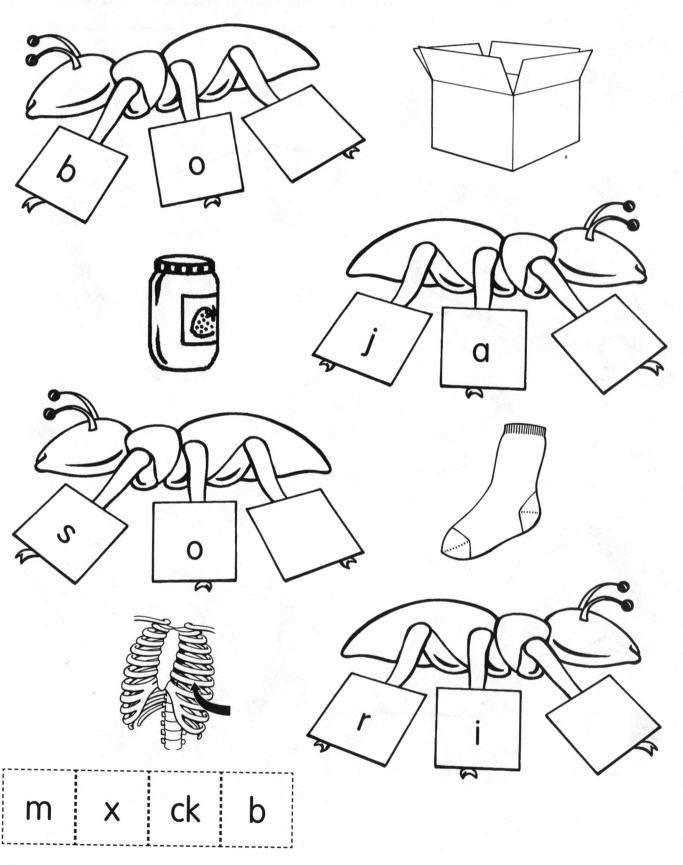

Words that begin with ch

Say the phoneme **ch**. Look at the pictures and say what they are. Some begin with **ch** and some don't. Cut out the words and stick them on the chart in the right place.

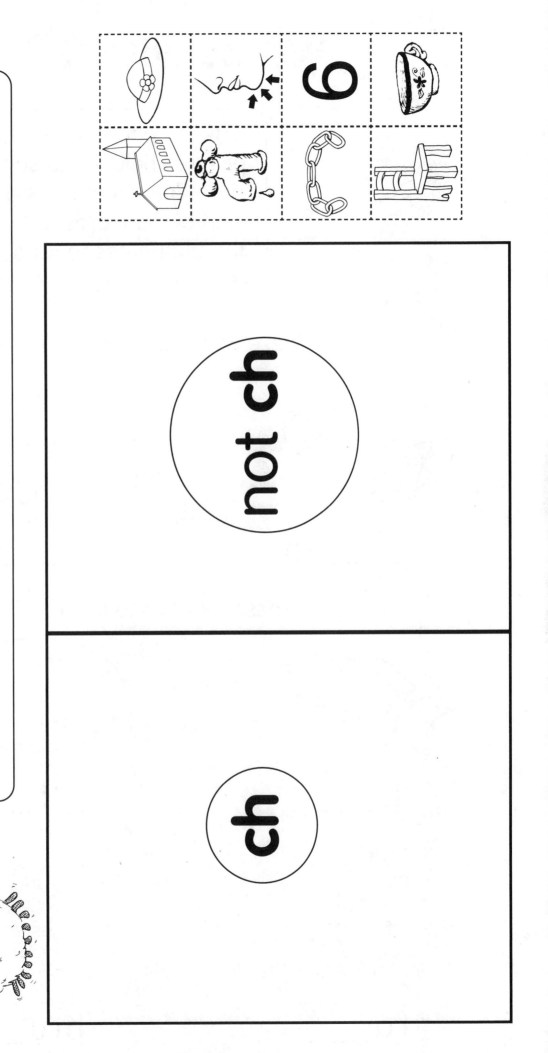

not ch

ch

Words with sh

sh

Say the phoneme **sh**. Look at the pictures below and say what they are. Write **sh** at the start or at the end of the words and then blend the phonemes to read the words.

These words start with sh

_____ ip

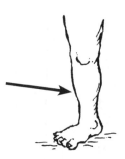

_____ in

These words end in sh

fi _____

di _____

ra _____

bru _____

Words that begin with **th**

Look at the words in the **th**under clouds.
Write **th** at the start of the words and then
blend the phonemes to read the words.

___in   ___ick

___ing   ___ink

___is   ___ank

___at   ___en

Words that begin with **qu**

Look at this word: | qu | ee | n |.

It begins with **qu**. Some of the words below begin with **qu**. Join the words that rhyme together.

| qu | eer |

| qu | ee | n |

| qu | i | ck |

| qu | a | ck |

| d | eer |

| s | i | ck |

| b | a | ck |

| b | ee | n |

The OW phoneme

Blend the phonemes to read the words. Can you hear the **ow** phoneme? It is sometimes spelt **ou**. Cut out the phonemes at the bottom of the page and stick them in the gaps to spell the words.

loud

shout

cow

town

clown

bow

| ow | ow | sh | ow | ow | ou | ou |
| b | l | n | c | t | d | n | t | l | c |

Words with oi

Blend the phonemes to read this word:

b	oi	l

It has the phoneme **oi**. Look at the pictures below and read the words. Cut them out and stick them together in pairs in the coins.

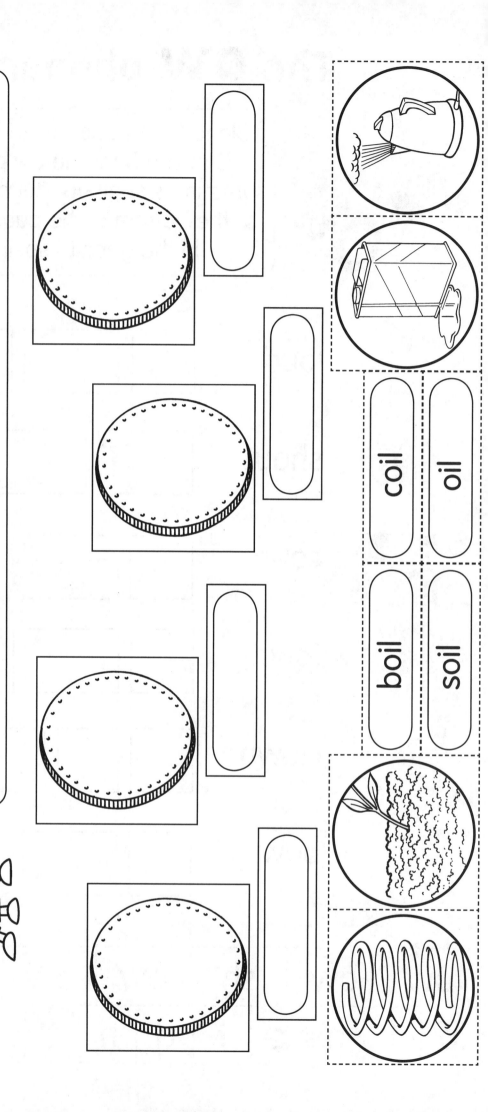

coil

oil

boil

soil

Words with **ar**

Look at the pictures below and say what they are. Blend the phonemes to read the words. Can you hear the phoneme **ar**? Join the pictures to the words.

star

car

jar

scar

bar

Add the first blend

Look at the pictures below and say what they are. Can you hear the blend at the start of each word? Say the blends in the rockets and then choose one to complete each word.

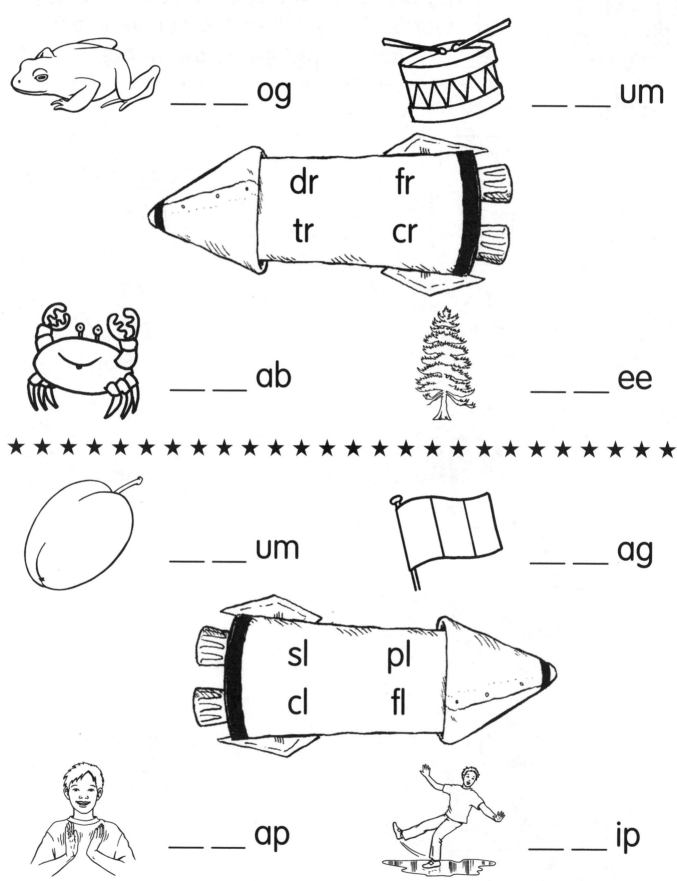

___ ___ og

___ ___ um

dr   fr
tr   cr

___ ___ ab

___ ___ ee

★ ★

___ ___ um

___ ___ ag

sl   pl
cl   fl

___ ___ ap

___ ___ ip

What is the first blend?

Look at the pictures below and say what they are. Three pictures in each flag show words that start with the same blend. Colour in these pictures and cross out the odd one.

tr

dr

pr

What is the first blend?

Look at the pictures and say what they are. Can you hear the blend at the start of each word? Blend the phonemes to read the words. Cut out the word that matches each picture and stick it underneath.

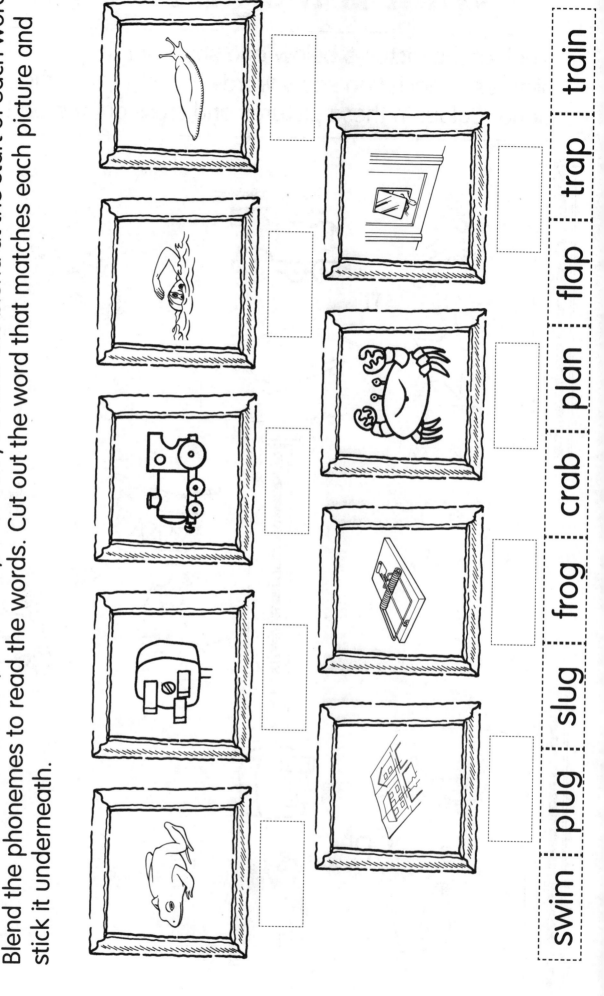

swim	plug	slug	frog	crab	plan	flap	trap	train

Simple nouns

Look at the things inside this house. Can you say what they are? Blend the phonemes to read the words. Cut out the words at the bottom of the page and stick them next to the objects in the house.

cup	tap	hat	jug	bed	bag
rug	pan	dish	cot	tin	clock

Answers

■ PAGE 5

| sad | sit |

| six 6 | sun |

■ PAGE 6

tap tin top

■ PAGE 7

pin pig pan

■ PAGE 8

nut
net
nun

■ PAGE 9

■ PAGE 10

sad sun

six sit

■ PAGE 11

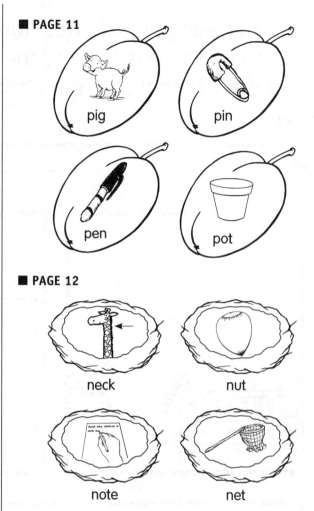

pig pin

pen pot

■ PAGE 12

neck nut

note net

■ PAGE 13

cat
cap
car
cot
cup

■ PAGE 14

hen

hat

hop

■ PAGE 15

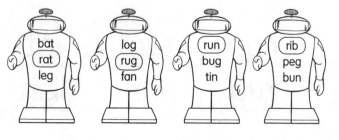

| bat rat leg | log rug fan | run bug tin | rib peg bun |

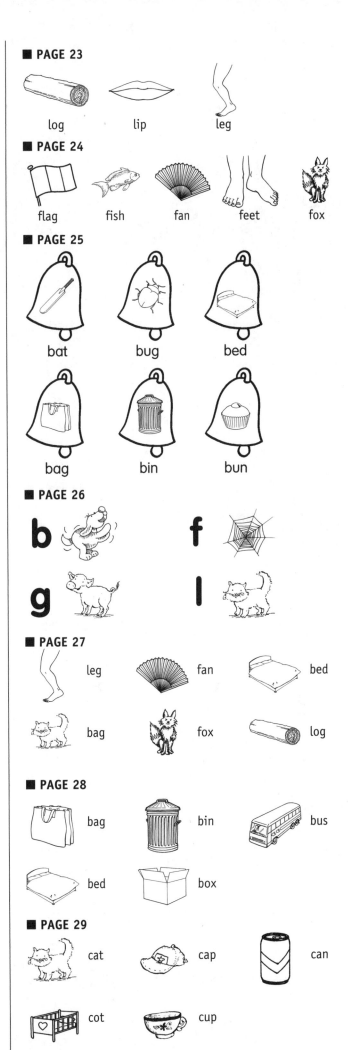

■ **PAGE 16**

mop   mug   mat

■ **PAGE 17**

dad
dig
dog
dot

■ **PAGE 18**

cat   rat   mop

dog   hat

■ **PAGE 19**

cap   cot

cut   cat

■ **PAGE 20**

hop

hen

hat   hot

■ **PAGE 21**

dad   dog

dig   dot

■ **PAGE 22**

goal   girl   goat   gate

■ **PAGE 23**

log   lip   leg

■ **PAGE 24**

flag   fish   fan   feet   fox

■ **PAGE 25**

bat   bug   bed

bag   bin   bun

■ **PAGE 26**

b   f

g   l

■ **PAGE 27**

leg   fan   bed

bag   fox   log

■ **PAGE 28**

bag   bin   bus

bed   box

■ **PAGE 29**

cat   cap   can

cot   cup

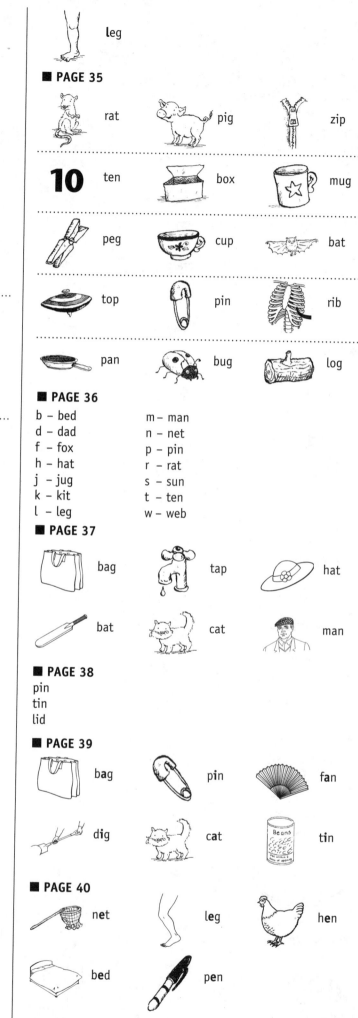

■ **PAGE 30**
fan
fin
fox

■ **PAGE 31**
hat
hen
hop
hot

■ **PAGE 32**

lip leg

lap log

pig pot

pan pen

man mug

map mop

■ **PAGE 33**

run rib rug

sad sun 6 six

top tap tin

■ **PAGE 34**

cat dog sun

pen bed tap

net cap bag

leg

■ **PAGE 35**

rat pig zip

10 ten box mug

peg cup bat

top pin rib

pan bug log

■ **PAGE 36**

b – bed   m – man
d – dad   n – net
f – fox   p – pin
h – hat   r – rat
j – jug   s – sun
k – kit   t – ten
l – leg   w – web

■ **PAGE 37**

bag tap hat

bat cat man

■ **PAGE 38**
pin
tin
lid

■ **PAGE 39**

bag pin fan

dig cat tin

■ **PAGE 40**

net leg hen

bed pen

■ PAGE 41

leg   rat   hat

net   pan   peg

■ PAGE 42

pig   hen   bed

web   dig

■ PAGE 43

cot   pot   dog

log

■ PAGE 44

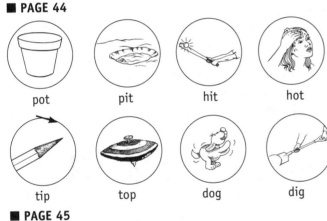

pot   pit   hit   hot

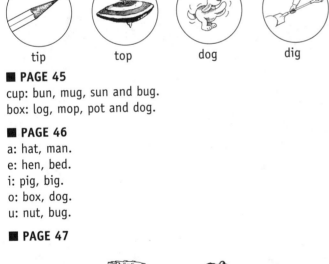

tip   top   dog   dig

■ PAGE 45

cup: bun, mug, sun and bug.
box: log, mop, pot and dog.

■ PAGE 46

a: hat, man.
e: hen, bed.
i: pig, big.
o: box, dog.
u: nut, bug.

■ PAGE 47

hat   bag   cap

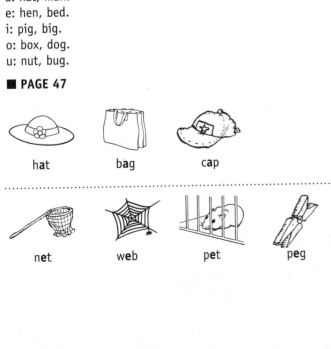

net   web   pet   peg

■ PAGE 48

bag   bug   pen   pin

top   tap   pit   pot

■ PAGE 49

bud   bag   pig   bed

jam   jog   jug   jet

■ PAGE 50

cap, dog, mop, web, pig, bug, map, tin, nut and net.

■ PAGE 51

rat   hat   cat

net   cot   mat

■ PAGE 52

cup   cap   mop

tap   pop   map

■ PAGE 53

pin   hen   fan

man   sun   pan

■ PAGE 54

n: pen.
p: cap, tap.
s: bus.
t: cat, nut.

■ PAGE 55

lick   sack   peck

■ PAGE 56
drum
plum
jam
pram

■ PAGE 57
bed
red
rod
lid
dad
bud
mud

■ PAGE 58
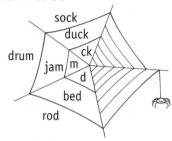

■ PAGE 59
 gu**n**

 ba**g**

 ta**p**

 le**g**

 pi**g**

 do**g**

■ PAGE 60
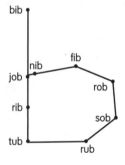

■ PAGE 61
jar: jam, jump, jelly and jug.

■ PAGE 62
w alien: wig, web and whale.
z alien: zip, zebra and zoo.

■ PAGE 63
 jam

 zip

 wig

 web

 jet

■ PAGE 64

d	g	n	p	t
red	mug	pen	hop	pet
bed	peg	hen	top	hot

■ PAGE 65
jug: dog, flag and frog.
sun: bin, hen and pen.

■ PAGE 66
 pan

 pin

 bed

 tap

 bin

 net

■ PAGE 67
 nail

 tail

 rain

 jail

 sail

■ PAGE 68
 boat

 soap

 coat

 toad

 goat

 road

■ PAGE 69
1. Apple **pie** is nice.
2. My dad wears a **tie**.
3. It is bad to **lie**.
4. I like meat **pie** and chips.
5. I **lie** down on my bed.
6. I can **tie** my laces.

■ PAGE 70
 bee

 sheep

3 three

 feet

 peel

■ PAGE 71
door

floor

four **4**

■ PAGE 72
 ring

 hang

song

fang

 king

 wing

ding dong

■ PAGE 73
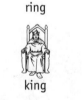 van

 vet

 vest

■ PAGE 74

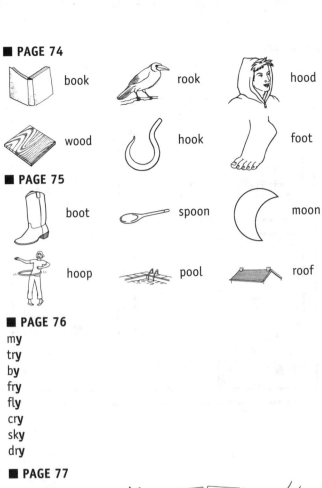

book · rook · hood

wood · hook · foot

■ PAGE 75

boot · spoon · moon

hoop · pool · roof

■ PAGE 76

m**y**
tr**y**
b**y**
fr**y**
fl**y**
cr**y**
sk**y**
dr**y**

■ PAGE 77

6

si**x** · fo**x** · bo**x** · mi**x**

■ PAGE 78

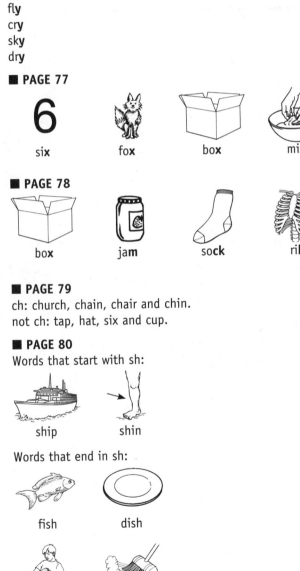

bo**x** · ja**m** · so**ck** · ri**b**

■ PAGE 79

ch: church, chain, chair and chin.
not ch: tap, hat, six and cup.

■ PAGE 80

Words that start with sh:

ship · shin

Words that end in sh:

fish · dish

rash · brush

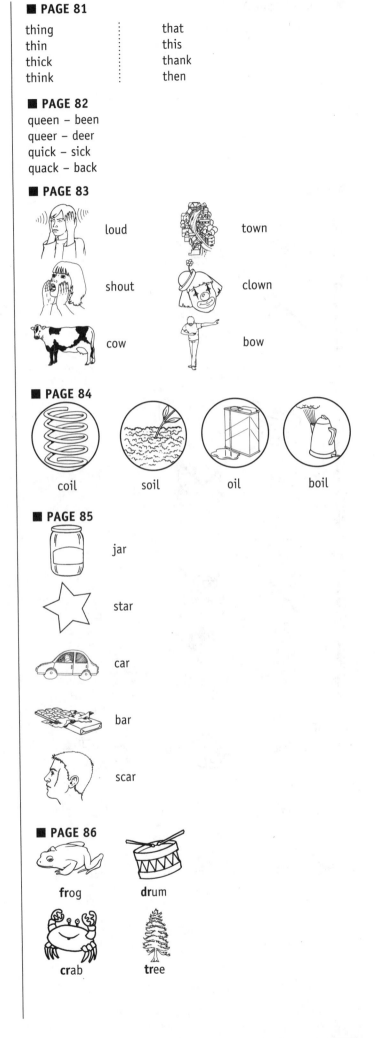

■ PAGE 81

thing that
thin this
thick thank
think then

■ PAGE 82

queen – been
queer – deer
quick – sick
quack – back

■ PAGE 83

loud · town

shout · clown

cow · bow

■ PAGE 84

coil · soil · oil · boil

■ PAGE 85

jar

star

car

bar

scar

■ PAGE 86

frog · **dr**um

crab · **tr**ee

plum   **fl**ag

 clap   **sl**ip

■ PAGE 87

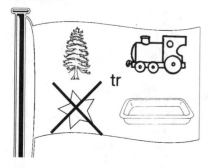

tr

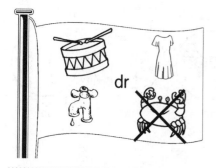

dr

pr

■ PAGE 88

 frog   plug   train

 swim   slug   plan

 trap   crab   flap

■ PAGE 89

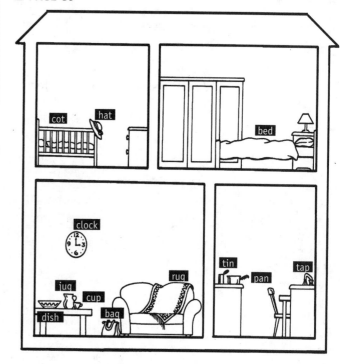

96